GOD WITHIN

GOD WITHIN
Our Spiritual Future—As Told by Today's New Adults

EDITED BY

JON M. SWEENEY,

EDITOR-IN-CHIEF, SKYLIGHT PATHS PUBLISHING

Walking Together, Finding the Way

SKYLIGHT PATHS PUBLISHING
WOODSTOCK, VERMONT

God Within:
Our Spiritual Future—As Told by Today's New Adults

Library of Congress Cataloging-in-Publication Data

God within : Our spiritual future—as told by today's new adults /
edited by Jon M. Sweeney & the editors at SkyLight Paths.
        p. cm.
Includes bibliographical references.
ISBN 1-893361-15-2
1. Spiritual life. 2. Youth—Religious life. I. Sweeney, Jon M., 1967– .
II. SkyLight Paths Publishing. III. Title.
BL624 .S695 2001
200'.84'2—dc21

                                                    2001002869

10 9 8 7 6 5 4 3 2 1

Manufactured in the United States of America

SkyLight Paths, "Walking Together, Finding the Way" and
colophon are trademarks of LongHill Partners, Inc.,
registered in the U.S. Patent and Trademark Office.

Walking Together, Finding the Way
Published by SkyLight Paths Publishing
A Division of LongHill Partners, Inc.
Sunset Farm Offices, Route 4, P.O. Box 237
Woodstock, VT 05091
Tel: (802) 457-4000   Fax: (802) 457-4004
www.skylightpaths.com

Contents

Introduction

JON M. SWEENEY,
EDITOR-IN-CHIEF, SKYLIGHT PATHS

TODAY'S NEW ADULTS

Like an old *Twilight Zone* flashback, imagine the world when you were eighteen. Were your teenage years marked by around the clock/around the globe instant media coverage? Did you watch or participate in extreme sports? (For that matter, could you see virtually any sporting event on the planet the same day that it was played?) In this time warp, imagine that attention-span-whittling real-life television, Playstation, and MTV are on the tube. You carry instant global communication and information in your pants pocket. When you need an answer to a question—How many Italian lira will it take to buy one euro? Is there a decent hotel room in midtown Manhattan available this weekend for less than $200? Does Christmas fall on a Monday or Friday this year?—you know in less than two minutes. You think less about where you are going than you do about what you are going to do on the way there. Your parents—who lived the excesses of the 1980s—and then started to sock it away in the '90s—are unsure of how to raise you. Why? Because their parents made a lot of mistakes in the late '60s and '70s when the old paradigms collapsed. The old adage—When in doubt of how to parent, do what your parents did; after all, you turned out okay—has worn out. This is a new day. If you can easily imagine yourself in these scenes than you just might be a New Adult.

"Young adults" are kids—sort of an amalgous term that we have often used in the past for post-pubescent boys and girls. "New adults" are men and women facing adult problems and questions at increasingly younger ages. Today's new adults can be as young as middle-teenagers; what makes them new—rather than young—is the speed with which they come of age.

God Within is a collection of singular voices representing thirteen different young women and men ages 17–25—new adults. At least five religious traditions are here, including Islam, Christianity, Buddhism, Wicca, and Judaism, plus a lot of spiritual searching completely outside of organized religion. There are two painters, one Rhodes Scholar, an agnostic, more than a few grassroots organizers, an on-line magazine editor, a divinity school student, a Ph.D., a witch-poet, a screenwriter and actor, a couple of retreat leaders, and much more.

It all began as a writing contest, a challenge. The editors at SkyLight Paths Publishing asked people across

America under the age of twenty-five: Tell us about your spiritual or religious life. Tell us how you see our spiritual present and future. We sent press releases to almost every college and university newspaper in the country. We asked hundreds of religion and literature professors to post announcements on departmental bulletin boards. We chatted the contest up on the Web. We even spammed a little. More than one hundred submissions eventually came in from twenty-nine different states over the course of six months, each earnest and smart. Our editors read them over and over again and finally decided on the pieces and authors that were best expressed and, as a whole, showed the widest range of spiritual and religious experience.

The results are remarkable. In memoir, story, poetry, and paintings, the contributors to *God Within* offer us a spiritual feast that is brutally honest and searing in insight. This is an early glimpse of what today's new adults—the so-called Generations X and Y—will bring to our spiritual expressions in the future. Remember their names, because we expect that in at least a few cases, you will be hearing from these authors again.

GENERATION WHAT?

Generations are slippery categories. Marketers, demographers, sociologists and media speak of the "Great" generation—the one that lived and thrived through the second world war; the "Lost" generation—either the bohemian expatriate American writers of the 1910s & 20s, or a derogative term for so-called Generation X, the confused children of baby boomers; the "Baby Boomer" generation—the richest and still the largest in recent history; the "Echo" generation— today's youngest people, also called Generation Y, and on and on. But rarely do the experts tell us why generation identity is supposed to build solidarity. Maybe it doesn't. Are generations really categories that their members take hold of?

Does proximity of birth year really make us more alike? How often do you hear someone say in everyday conversation, "As a member of Generation [fill in the blank], I think...." Or, "You obviously don't understand my generation"? Talk like that is less common than talk like this: "A certain amount of life-experience is necessary to understand what I'm talking about" or "He's too old to get it." Too often, generations become ghettos for our own assumptions.

Maturity has always been measured in time and space. The substance of one's character and the range of one's understanding were determined, in large part, by age and exposure—the older you were, and the more you encountered, the more mature you became. These time and space continuums are becoming much shorter for today's new adults. They are challenging many of our assumptions, and for good reasons.

But there is very little in *God Within* by way of signposts of generation identity. If you have come to this book for answers to sociological questions—"Why do those teenagers do what they do?"—you had better look elsewhere. The message from our contributors is that you cannot understand an abstract called a generation, but if you listen to one of these new adults for a time you may come to understand more about yourself—because theirs is the vision of the future.

WE ARE ALL CHILDREN OF OUR PARENTS

There are socio-political-economic facts that distinguish today's generation under twenty-five from their parents. Most significantly, today's new adults have grown up with less organized religion than has any American generation before them. Even though previous generations have had the same spiritual impulses—for seeking, wandering, faithfulness, and rebellion—today's new adults can freely become spiritual explorers in ways that their parents could not.

But the collapse of organized religion as the dominant, normative spiritual force in people's lives is not the sole reason why we have such a variety of spiritual expression today. As you read this book, you will discover that to come to such a conclusion gives religion both too much, and too little, credit. For today's new adults, "organized religion" is simply one treatment for the same sickness we all have shared from time to time throughout the ages. The spiritual emptiness that ails each of us (some of us more often than others) does not find a simple cure in organized religion today any more than it did yesterday. The difference is: Today, we are more free to admit it and find alternatives, correctives, and additives. For this reason, the contributors to *God Within* often express the antithesis of spiritual emptiness—almost a spiritual overflow.

If there is a trend to be found in the following pages, it is in the confident responses of today's 17–25 year olds to the spiritual confusion of their parents. The contributors to *God Within* show impatience in dealing with leaders of any kind who are continually unsure, unreflective, and do not understand the impact their decisions have on the broader world around them. We can even see this in simple brands and marketing. Powerful names like Levi's and Nike have taken nose-dives in the past several years as today's emerging consumers are unimpressed by what they perceive to be their unenlightened appeals to style and power to sell their product. Today's new adults want what's real, necessary, and what makes a difference. Lindsay Keipper, one of the contributors to *God Within*, says "We hunger for honesty. The world is a liar and a cheat, and we rebel against that because we believe in something better. We want the truth, but the world is a liar and a cheat, and she will try to cheat us into becoming liars too." (p. 11)

Aren't today's new adults also supposed to feel antagonistic and powerless in the face of authority, dogma, and institutions? Not necessarily—the world is changing and so have young Americans' response to it. The vagaries of James Dean-like angst and rebellion, so adored by the parents of today's new adults, may finally be passing. The powerlessness we feel in trying to fight corruption and authoritarianism may be changing, too. Today's new adults react differently than their parents once did; there is more pragmatism; there is much more to get done. Also, there are fewer tangible things to fight against; our enemies are more subtle, often cloaked.

Today's young adults are shaping themselves to become our rebellion against what is mediocre, half-baked, and without earnest—and we should thank them for it. Without this kind of rebellion we would remain primitive people. We would be listening to the wrong voices, or simply too often content with the status quo. The fight against ordinariness begins in unhappiness and dissatisfaction. These attitudes are worlds apart from simple angst.

The parents of our contributors made popular the spiritual movements and institutions of today: Buddhist meditation, Jewish Renewal, yoga centers, Habitat for Humanity, Centering Prayer, Earth Day and other avenues of environmental awareness, and many others. It will be interesting to watch for the spiritual movements of the next fifty years.

DEBUNKING THE DABBLING MYTH

Over the past decade, sociologists and less forgiving religionists have written of the new "cafeteria-style approach" to religion. We are a people today, they conclude, who have lost our moorings in organized religion and are adrift in a sea of spiritual opportunities. These opportunities have never been more available or as diverse as they are today. More than ever before, people of different religious traditions are combined in the workplace, our communities, and even our families. And so—confronted with the collapse of organized religion and the great opportunities for learning and experiencing other spiritual paths—we dabble a bit in yoga, we meditate in different traditions, we pray, and we move from one spiritual group to another freely. There is no longer a connection between spiritual growth and religious commitment.

Our contributors show a different picture for the future. Today's new adults form the most diverse generation in history. Today's twenty-year-old is twice as likely as her parents to identify herself as multiethnic. It is more difficult today to narrowly define distinct socio-economic or racial groups. We don't huddle together as much as we used to. We aggressively break down tribal mentalities. For example, for the first time in history, today's teenagers are growing up in an environment where it is broadly accepted to come out of the closet. Sexual and other orientations lead less often than ever before to isolation. This affects our spirituality.

Today's new adult is not always dabbling when she combines various spiritual practices into her own. She is often expressing the spiritual impulses of the various places from where she comes. Today's new adults are more naturally familiar with those things that their parents only dabble(d) in. What we might interpret as casual interest is really something much deeper. Sociologist Wade Clark Roof dubbed the Baby Boomers "a generation of seekers" in 1993. *God Within* shows us a set of voices that are doing less seeking and more...creating.

Today's new adults may most accurately be called a generation of spiritual creators.

THE TRADITION TURNAROUND

The meaning of spiritual identity is changing. Our contributors are breaking down the boundaries of religion—and it feels completely natural to them. Organized religion is still meaningful, but it is not the definition of personal, spiritual identity. Whereas their parents could easily say: "I am a Christian" or "I am a Muslim"; today it is a bit more complicated. These words of traditional identity don't come to the lips as easily as they used to.

Terms such as "conversion" and "faithfulness" are losing their religious meaning too, because they so rarely explain people's experiences of spirituality today. To be a part of one religious tradition does not preclude you from joining another spiritual movement. For example, many of today's young evangelical Christians might feel completely comfortable in a hatha yoga class—but this does not mean that their ministers will understand. As Eboo Patel, one of the contributors to *God Within*, writes: "My generation lives at the crossroads of inheritance and discovery. We are

Muslims who admire the Dalai Lama and Christians who talk about karma. Our challenge is to be true to ancient traditions while living fully on the frontiers of modernity." (p. 152)

Each of the ruthlessly honest contributions to this slim book should provoke thoughts of your own, should force you to consider your spiritual identity in new ways. You may find, like the artist Gwyneth Tripp, that this process of self-searching is like "being at the edge of something powerful but completely unknown—feeling innocent, curious, strong, and cautious about what one might step into." (p. 48)

1

Love and Strategy

EBOO PATEL

"We wake, if we ever wake at all, to mystery. . ."
—ANNIE DILLARD

There were a few empty seats on the eastbound Circle Line train at Victoria Station—a rare occurrence for evening rush hour in London. It made the person responsible for the odor easier to identify. The content of the smell was old, sour sweat, and maybe a little urine. You don't smell that way after playing basketball in the hot sun, or even after three days camping without a shower.

He was white, thirtyish, wore a New York Yankees baseball cap. I watched him eat a banana. He took the peel off, placed it behind him, held the fruit in his hand, and bit jaggedly into the flesh. I thought to myself, his hands probably aren't clean. Bits of banana clung to the hair on his face.

The train stopped, and a well-groomed man boarded and sat in the empty seat next to him. He noticed the odor, glanced at the source with disgust, and shrank away.

The first man finished his banana and stood up, walked toward me, threw his bag on the floor, sat down next to it, and said, "It's not me, okay mate, it's my trainers."

Oh no, I thought; this nut is gonna get angry and start a fight. I decided that I would get into another train car at the next stop. I returned to my mindscape of upcoming appointments and looming deadlines. Then I looked at him again.

He was staring at the floor, or maybe at his shoes. And it occurred to me that he didn't look like a nut. It occurred to me that I didn't know where the smell on his shoes came from. I had a hard time imagining it—how would they get that smelly, why wouldn't he change them?

And I realized that I was surprised that this man got angry. When someone falls so low that they smell up a train and put their dirty hands on the fruit of a banana in public, then do they have the right to get angry when well-groomed people stare at them with disgust and shrink away?

And suddenly I am seeing myself. I am hearing the story I have been telling myself. I am studying my rationale for wanting to move to another part of the train. I am wishing I were less low, less ugly, less weak. Why did I think this man should respond to an insult with any less anger than I would?

I stayed on the train and saw him pick up his bags and move to another empty seat. He leaned forward and began peeling another banana. The cap hid his eyes. But I thought I saw them anyway. I know that look, I said to myself.

Staying on the train was no great act of justice or mercy or generosity on my part. Still, it was a small victory in the *jihad-al-nafs*: the holy war against the lower self. My first instinct was to leave, and I stayed. My first instinct was to turn away, and I looked again. My first instinct was to wipe him from my consciousness, and now he is part of my being.

Listen to this story, and you will understand why what I write is about spirituality. A young Yeshiva student was going to see a great rabbi. His friends asked him, "Will you ask the *rebbe* about the Torah?" The student said, "No." They asked, "Will you discuss the Talmud with the *rebbe*?" The student said, "No." "Then why are you going?" they wondered. The student responded, "I want to see how the *rebbe* ties his shoes."

I learn more about Islam every day. Some of it is from the books I have to read for my dissertation in the sociology of religion. Most of it is in the moments I catch myself being less of a Muslim than I ought to be.

I used to say that I pray to say "Thank You" and to ask for help. Now I know that there is at least one more reason. I want to rewire myself, to transform my first instinct. Instead of having a first instinct to leave, to turn away, or to wipe from my consciousness, I want my first instinct to be to stay, to witness, to absorb into my being.

When I first read Freemon Dyson's book *Disturbing the Universe* in college, I was floored by his idea of cosmic unity—that we are all part of the same fabric, and that when somebody else is hurt, I am hurt too. I began to imagine the suffering of hungry children, soldiers in war, abused women. Then I became too sophisticated to care about other people's suffering. "Compassion is a waste of energy," I wrote a friend, "because it clouds strategic thinking."

And now I care about strategy in basketball. And in the rest of my life, I am trying to be good.

Eboo Patel is the executive director of the Interfaith Youth Core. He has worked as an artist, a teacher, and an organizer on four continents. He has given speeches with luminaries such as Raimon Pannikar and Huston Smith, and at venues such as UNESCO in Paris and the Parliament of the World Religions in Cape Town, South Africa. Eboo is a Rhodes Scholar completing a doctorate in the sociology of religion at Oxford University.

Influences of mine . . .

One book: *Their Eyes Were Watching God,* by Zora Neale Hurston

One album: *Stop Making Sense,* by The Talking Heads

One spiritual leader: Prophet Muhammad (peace be upon him)

One artist: Rumi

One thinker: Paulo Freire

2

Simply Complicated

LINDSAY KEIPPER

I am a child of steadfast faith, loyal family and friends, and secure future becoming an adult with no direction, no shoulders to lean on, and no God. Once upon a time, I thought I had found everything I needed to make my life complete. I thought I knew who I was—a writer, a Christian, a person who mattered in the grand scheme of things. In a few short months, my God abandoned me, my writer's inspiration fled, and I found myself without a career or a spiritual truth to stand on.

How did this happen? I'm afraid that if you read on hoping for answers, or a moral, or a trite conclusion that melts on your tongue like a piece of maple candy, you will be disappointed. I have no solid answers to offer you, because I still haven't figured them out for myself.

FIGURING OUT WHO I AM

I am a member of a generation of kids set adrift by parental detachment, single motherhood, a poor educational system, relativistic attitudes, and too much violence on TV. That's what the media say, anyway. But you could open a newspaper if you wanted to know about the latest stereotypes. What I truly am is harder to pin down. I can't turn the story of all that has shaped and molded who I am into a sound bite. I don't even want to, because it's really an insult to think you can pin a person down with a single phrase or slogan. The other problem with stating who I am is that I'm not quite sure.

I can tell you who I was. I grew up in a Christian home, attending Lutheran churches and Sunday schools and learning that Jesus loves me and the Bible tells me so. When I grew a bit more spiritually mature during high school, and started doubting my faith and the principles that I had been taught were true, my sense of who I was became more than a little shaky. My grandmother was dying of cancer, my soul was dying of bitterness and cynicism, and my faith was dying of doubt. I spent almost two years in spiritual limbo, wondering just what this alleged God thought he was playing at.

I have moments when I feel as if I'm the only person on earth who has suffered through this sort of depression, but in moments of lucidity, I have to admit that I am often the Generation Y angst poster girl. Our generation has been

characterized by suicidal tendencies and the bouts of violent depression a lot of us seem to have experienced. It's
true that no generalization is true for everyone all of the
time. However, the fact is that when I relate my stories of
spiritual doubt and depression to my peers, far more of
them are nodding in understanding than are staring in
shock. Suicidal tendencies aside, I believe that every
human being goes through at least one period in his or her
life when every value, every moral, every article of faith in
his or her spiritual repertoire comes under fire.

This is not a fun process.

The urge to define ourselves and our world, to line
everything up in rows and explain it logically, is a funda-
mental part of human beings. That's what we call reason,
and why we consider ourselves superior to other animals.
Religion evolved out of this quest for definition. Even now,
as science claims to have displaced religion as the rational
explainer of life, religion remains important because it
answers questions science can't. Science may tell us what
the world is made of and how it works, but science can't
explain the meaning of life or tell us what happens when we
die. We need religion, and so we are devastated when the
spiritual aspects of our life come into doubt and we no
longer have any explanations to cling to.

This questioning of faith isn't all bad, because in the
long run, seeking the truth is a positive thing. It may hurt to
turn on our long-trusted beliefs and feel unable to follow
them any longer, but this is the only way we can know

whether the belief we follow is essentially true or false. This is important to know, largely because this is the only real way to ferret out the problems in the established systems of religion, society, and government. When we question the sincerity of our faith, we question the systems that spawned that faith. And if we don't like what we find, we know it's time for a change. There are people who are so entrenched in their own worldview that they're totally unshakable. They are totally blind to the problems they cause, and in a way I can't entirely blame them, because when we don't question ourselves we lose all sense of perspective.

When your beliefs are rocked to the core, you may end up denying your faith and moving on, or you may end up believing in your principles more strongly than before. Either way, your beliefs become a little more sincere, and the world becomes a little more honest.

I was made stronger by doubt. I came back to Christianity more fervent than before, convinced that I could hear God speaking to me and see him working through my life. It was only when I arrived at college that things began to change. For a while, I continued to feel that I knew exactly who I was and what I believed, but at some point, there was a change. All of a sudden, church had become a torment, and I no longer felt like talking to God. Even more frightening, I didn't really feel too concerned that my faith had disappeared.

The apathy startled me more than the doubt. Where was the passion I had felt just a few months before? And why, when I made myself face the issues troubling me, was I filled with such bitterness? This wasn't mere questioning of God's existence; this was questioning of God's motives.

The source of my problem with God was a long night when I was still new to college. That night, I found myself unable to sleep, scared by something unseen that I could not explain or identify. Okay, maybe I had spent too much time in the Christian bookstore's charismatic section, but as I was seized by wave after wave of abject terror, I became convinced that I was under demonic attack. I was all alone in the room, my family and friends were hours away, and the only one who could come to my aid, I was convinced, was God. I prayed, I rebuked, I called, I begged. But this isn't the 700 Club, and I think you can guess how this little tale ends.

I never consciously acknowledged that I had been abandoned until months later, when my mind suddenly stumbled over this scene as the reason for my loss of faith. It was then that I was forced to be honest with myself and ask whether the entire source of my spiritual problems might be that I was simply pissed off at God.

HONESTY, MY CREED

If you get the impression that I'm hung up on honesty, you're absolutely correct. At some point in my life, I decided that I'm the only one who knows enough about my mind to understand or explain what's going on inside it. That's where honesty comes in. If people are going to know me, judge me, or just disdain me, I want them to know or judge or disdain who I really am, not some shallow exterior. I want to be a genuine person, and I want the person that everyone sees to be the deepest part of myself. I screw up sometimes because I don't always know who I really am, but at the bottom of my moral code, I am forbidden to misrepresent or delude myself.

The problem in situations like this is that I don't want to believe what may be the truth about this whole unpleasant ordeal. I don't want to think that the pain and loneliness I'm going through are my own fault for having wrong assumptions and stubborn pride. I don't want to think that I'm being slowly drawn back into Christianity, despite the fact that I don't know how I feel about it, yet. And I especially don't want to think that if neither of these things is true, God is dead or indifferent and I am alone. But because of honesty, my eternal credo, if I conclude that these unpleasant things are true, I must admit them to myself, and I must admit them to other people.

This is the great struggle of people in the so-called Generation Y. We are fighting for honesty and genuine representation of self in a world where self-delusion seems to be the only way to survive.

We are confronted by an array of choices and problems. At the same time, centuries-old prejudices and belief structures are continuing to fall away, and the once taboo is becoming fashionable. Humanity as a whole is becoming painfully aware of how many problems we have caused and how high the stakes are when it comes to fixing them. We are a generation that grew up knowing, for the most part, that we are all created equal, and that if we surmount the obstacles we can all end up in the same exalted place. The world certainly isn't perfect—a fact of which we are painfully aware—but there are more career and spiritual paths available for all of us than ever before. We are also a generation that grew up knowing exactly how screwed up the world is. Violence, crime, pollution, poverty—we can't ignore them any longer because we all know that they're there.

As a group, we hunger for honesty. The world is a liar and a cheat, and we rebel against that because we believe in something better. We want the truth, but the world is a liar and a cheat, and she will try to cheat us into becoming liars too.

Human beings want answers. We want quick, simple answers that can be implemented immediately. We want results. We have trouble coping when there are no easy answers. And in cases where an easy answer will not suffice, we create one anyway and pretend that it does. Got a problem with crime? Reforming our country's systems of health care, education, and criminal justice is just too complicated, so we'd better just build more prisons and mandate stricter sentencing. Got a problem with school violence? Human beings are too insanely complex to bother trying to figure out, so we'd better just limit the sale of guns and put the Ten Commandments up in our schools.

When we're faced with a problem of staggering intensity, it's simpler to delude ourselves into believing that a few easy steps will make it all okay than to admit that we need to reform our society entirely. People of Generation Y look at the world's problems and say, "This is some messed-up shit. We need some major reforms here." Right now we are young, and we are idealistic. We want something better for our future. What we want is honesty.

We want people who are deluding themselves this way to wake up and see that their self-delusion may be making life easier for them, but it's making the problems they're ignoring worse. We want corporations and politicians to tell us the truth. We want them to own up and stop feeding us garbage. We don't want the world to kneel to us; we just want to be respected to the point where people don't try to lie to us. It seems to be true of American society that each generation as a whole becomes more aware and more open to different ideas than the generation before. But I am afraid that as we go out into the world and try to change it, we will become so overwhelmed by the immensity of the world's problems that we will simply give up and lapse into self-delusion, wasting all our potential in the most selfish manner possible.

Voter turnout is low, especially among the younger generations. Why do you think that is? If you think that the reason is apathy in young people, you have been duped by the popular press. We care about the world and its problems. We care deeply. The problem is that we are losing hope, because we look at the rest of the world going about its business, we look at politicians smiling and lying, we look at corporations stuffing those politicians' pockets with money, and we look at the same problems coming up over and over and over again and never getting solved. We may disagree on how these problems should be solved, but we can all see the self-delusion and the bullshit, and we are sick and tired of it. If everyone is a liar, our only option is to divorce ourselves from the system that spawned those liars.

I believe this is why more and more people are turn-ing to atheism and agnosticism as answers. We are over-whelmed by a plethora of religious options, and it's hard to sort out what we believe. We are less willing than previous generations to say, "I don't really agree with this stuff, but this was how I was raised, so I guess I'll stick with this reli-gion." We are reluctant to commit until we're sure that we really believe what we're going to say we believe. As a result, when we can't be sure what it is that we really be-lieve, the only truly honest way is to say, "I don't know what I believe. I can't follow your God, so I guess I have no God."

We feel lost and alone when we have no answers, when we can't explain why life is the way it is. Even and especially when the world is so messed up, it's important to believe that what we do matters and that there is some-thing else besides the endless pain and frustration of trying to figure things out. I believe, and I think many of my peers agree, that it's better to stand alone than to dedicate your faith to a belief or cause you're not really sure is right.

When I say I worship God, am I really saying that I worship a being that pretends to love the world while only caring for himself? I ask myself, "If this God is the selfish maniac he appears to be, how can I spend my entire life worshiping him? What a waste of a life that I could dedicate to something better."

I am learning what many of my peers have already discovered: my views on spirituality and God do not have to be limited by what I have been taught up to this point. Spirituality can go far beyond religion, if we let it.

I think that at times, older generations have a tendency to assume that the apparent lack of protests and marches and fist-waving these days means that Generation Y is apathetic or that its members have nothing to contribute to the world. I disagree.

I think our contribution is slightly more subtle. It's not always evident in what we say and do in public, but it's there, in our attitude and in our belief system. It is evident in our craving for honesty and, perhaps more importantly, in our ability to see that spirituality doesn't have to be contained by religion. The impact of these qualities goes far beyond personal faith. You may call me an overzealous idealist, but I believe that openness and honesty, while perhaps not the most obvious agents of change, will do more and better work in the world than close-mindedness and lying.

The changes we make may happen more often behind the scenes than in the streets, but once we're through, the world will never be the same.

Lindsay Keipper *is a college student and aspiring writer who spends her time attending classes, reading science fiction novels, and neglecting her assorted web pages. After graduating from Pennsylvania State University, she hopes to pursue a career as either a lawyer or an FBI agent. While Lindsay's spiritual life may need a bit of sorting out, she is blessed with a loving family, wonderful friends, and extremely cute pets. When she's not at Penn State learning about uniform crime reports, she lives in Frederick, Maryland.*

Influences of mine . . .

One book: The World According to Garp, by John Irving

One album: Wise Man's Tragedy, by Solomon's Wish

One spiritual leader: Jesus Christ

One artist: Kevin Eastman and Peter Laird

One thinker: Immanuel Kant

3

Two Stars

ELIZABETH OCHS

*H*er track uniform wrinkling to the beat, Lanny belted out, "No fame or fortune, no riches untold," and the other girls in the locker room responded, "I'd rather have Jesus than silver or gold." Voices of the track team burst out. Shoes started stomping, and lockers thumped to the beat. This was intense. This was no longer a locker room. This was the black church, and it had come to meet a Jewish sprinter standing in the corner smiling.

After going to a private Jewish day school in suburban New Jersey for ten years, I had come to a public high school in Charlottesville, Virginia. I believed I was coming to the Deep South. I was ready for the grits. I was ready for the southern accents and cows. Instead, I ended up in a town just like the North but with a few more hills and slower stoplights. There were, however, a whole lot fewer Jews. I was the foreigner. For this I was not prepared.

In New Jersey, being Jewish for me meant being part of the community. Now in Charlottesville, at times, being Jewish means separating myself from the community. My family has always loosened our religious rules in order to take part in a non-Jewish society. Yet, we've made our decisions privately, not to set an example but to deal with our situation. Following our family tradition, I had planned to privately discover what it meant to be Jewish in Charlottesville. Instead, by being part of a team, every action I would now take would be what Jewish people do. Every random thought I expressed would become what Jewish people believe. At first I wanted to hide. How could I explain why I couldn't go to track meets on Saturdays—days when I observed my Sabbath? How could I make my answers so absolute when I wasn't sure myself?

I began to explain that from sunset on Friday night, until at least three stars appear in the sky on Saturday night, I don't drive, work, or spend money. Sabbath provides me with a day of rest, a day to accept what is around me and not create nor acquire more. But how could I practice running week after week and not go to track meets? On one hand, fully plunging into my religious observances would mean letting my team down. On the other hand, going to every Saturday track meet would mean losing a day that I need to recharge spiritually and mentally.

I tried to accommodate both. For instance, when track meets were out of town, I drove there the night before so that I could walk to the track the next morning. I told myself that there is such thing as a Sabbath track meet day to praise God through the power of the body. Still, Friday nights lost their restfulness, their family-ness, and their holiness. And as I warmed up for the 55-meter dash Saturday morning, sweat and stomach cramps pushed me far from prayers. I began to learn that I could not live perfectly in two separate worlds. They would have to merge, stretch, and pull, each giving and letting go.

As the bus bumped home, Ebony, Lanny, and I leaned against each other with the relief of the state meet's ending. After singing all the oldies songs we knew, the next song that came up was the locker room favorite, "I'd Rather Have Jesus than Silver and Gold." Sing along, I told myself; go ahead and sing about Jesus. You won't be struck by lightning.

"Hey, what's your God's name?" Ebony asked between verses.

"Well, um, his name is Hashem," I answered.

Lanny joined in, "I'd rather have Hashem than silver and gold . . ." The song continued, only with greater warmth. I realized that although we sang from different backgrounds and headed home to different lives, we could find common spirit. Riding home that Saturday night, I saw only two stars in the sky, but our blended voices brought me to the third.

Elizabeth Ochs *is a senior at Charlottesville High School in Charlottesville, Virginia. She lives with two parents and two cats and a sister. She enjoys running, modern dance, writing, and community service. Within the Jewish community she teaches, tutors, studies, and leads services.*

Influences of mine . . .

One book: *Franny and Zooey*, by J. D. Salinger, has influenced me not because it has given me any answers but because it has supported me in my questioning.

One album: *Brushfire Fairytales* by Jack Johnson is funky, lively, and has great lyrics, including "Slow down, you're moving too fast . . ." (something we all need to hear).

One spiritual leader: Morah Devorah Benisti. Whoever said that your kindergarten teacher couldn't teach you about life? Judaism gained a kind and thoughtful face because of her.

One artist: Charlottesville dancers Micki Liszt and members of the Zen Monkey Project. These dancers are not only creative and innovative but strive to mentor young dancers.

One thinker: Henry David Thoreau and Abraham Joshua Heschel.

4

Nestled in the Lap of the Goddess

PAMELA DAWN deFOREST

I am twenty-one years old and a senior at the University of Redlands in southern California. I am studying museum studies, history, and creative writing. I am a Witch.

I grew up in a house divided by spiritual beliefs. My mother was a Christian Scientist, and she clung to it with such fervor that no matter how much pain she was in, she refused to seek any medical attention. My father, on the other hand, abandoned any sense of spirituality because he had so much hate pent up inside, and he resorted to becoming a Nazi. At the same time he was a hypochondriac and went to the doctor several times a month. Because of those extreme opposites, the house was in a constant whirlwind of fights and emotional distress. I suffered immensely because I couldn't completely accept what my mother believed, and I didn't believe in anything my father did.

I spent most if not all of my time with my mom, and she was always very wrapped up in her religious beliefs. She woke up early every morning to read *Science & Health* (the Christian Science companion to the Bible). She would pray over me whenever I was sick, and she tried so hard to be a good person according to her religion. I think that my mother wouldn't have been able to get through most of her life without her beliefs. Because of my mom's strength through that faith, I always felt the need to hold onto and create a spiritual path of my own.

I went to Sunday school for many years and still couldn't accept what the Bible said. I couldn't understand the wrathful God of the Old Testament and didn't agree with the roles set for women in the New Testament. Then there was the addition of the odd concepts brought forth by Mary Baker Eddy (the creator of Christian Science), with her idea of evil not being real, and that it's in your mind so you can get rid of it with prayer. All of these concepts forced me to always ask questions, and because of my overly inquisitive nature I was put into a Sunday school class all by myself. My teacher was an older man who was willing to put up with me. I think he found it refreshing to deal with a child who wanted to learn more. But when he couldn't answer all of my questions, like "Why is 'God' a man in the Bible?" I eventually just gave up and stopped going altogether.

Another force in my life was trying to mold me but also couldn't answer any of my questions. I went to a

Reborn Christian school from kindergarten through the twelfth grade. This made me truly not believe in the biblical God. I couldn't allow myself to follow a religion that had killed so many people, damned you to hell if you didn't believe, and was so entirely filled with hypocrites.

I had always seen myself as a spiritual person, but I just didn't know how to connect with the wonderful power that I saw everywhere—in the plants in my grandmother's garden, or in the lake where I spent my summers, or in myself. The God I had been educated about didn't live in any of those things. I was taught that he was up in heaven, looking down on us and controlling our lives. He wasn't any real part of what I considered spiritual. So I began to think that what I felt was wrong, but I still knew it was so real and powerful. Because I felt that religion was so important, and because I didn't believe in the one I had grown up with, I became very depressed.

Throughout those years of anguish I tried to find information about other belief systems in the hope that I could finally find peace. I don't remember exactly when I first became interested in earth-based religions—but I do remember thinking as a child that the Native American religion made more sense than anything I had been formally taught. It was the first belief system I knew of that saw nature as holy. From there, I learned about the Druids and was also fascinated with gypsies, healing stones, and anything supernatural. And then, when I was thirteen years old,

I met a Witch in a bulletin board chat room on my computer and knew that I had found someone like me. It felt like coming home to myself for the first time.

My parents finally allowed me to become a student of this wonderful lady when I was around 15. But before that, I read everything about the Craft that I could get my hands on. Through these two tools—as well as just going out into nature and drinking in all the energy and knowledge that the great Earth would allow me to consume—I began to learn about what it was I had always believed in.

I was so happy to find a belief system that recognized all the things I found sacred. I finally understood why I collected rocks from streams and leaves from the apple tree in our neighbor's yard, and why I set up little altars everywhere. I understood why I felt so invigorated when the wind blew down off the mountain and enfolded me. It was revealed that the energies I had always considered sacred really were.

CREATING A BELIEF SYSTEM FOR MYSELF

In all of this I found the Goddess, and I began to develop my own path. Believing in a deity as feminine made me feel comfortable and strong. I no longer had to fear a god or question his teaching, because what I was learning all made sense.

This is the belief system I have created for myself: I believe that the world was created by, and is a part of, a beautiful and strong feminine force that shaped all things that exist out of Herself. I believe in Magic and that you can shape the world around you by tapping into that Force. I do that by crafting spells and utilizing the powers of the elements, which is what magic and everything else around us is composed of. However, I am careful not to invoke energy that would wrongly affect anyone or anything. I am cautious because the code of the Craft is that whatever you do comes back to you threefold.

I also believe in reincarnation and that you go on to the next life after you learn what you need in this one. Eventually you just go back to Her, because we are all a part of the Divine anyway. However, you must learn and create, love and live in order to understand how you fit into Her. Essentially, we are all a part of everything and are everything at once. Our lives are just the journey to find out where we belong in the puzzle.

I don't think that the beliefs I have constructed for myself are that different from what my mom truly believes. She feels that you should care for people and be without judgment, and that whatever you do comes back to you. I really feel she has a little magic of her own. I think that because of me and my beliefs, my mom has questioned the beliefs she grew up with and has also built a belief system of her own. My dad has also

changed a lot since I was little. He still has a lot of anger
and frustration pent up inside of him, but I have allowed
him to see another side of spirituality that is more open.
I think that some of the hate he felt was because he didn't
have a connection with anything divine. Now, he knows
more—so he's growing just as I am, but in the way that he
needs to.

Ever since I was sixteen my spiritual path has played
an extremely important role in my life. In fact, it is my life. I
have infused everything with my own sort of magic. I use
tarot cards to show me where I am on my journey and gather insight on where I need to be. I have turned my home
into a completely sacred space. I have altars in every room
that help me to direct Her energy into my life. I decorate
with gifts from nature such as stones and dried herbs, and I
have a fountain in my living room to utilize the energy of
water—which is love and emotion. I wear jewelry that helps
me channel the natural forces I need in my life, such as a
bone Goddess necklace to remind me that She is always
with me, and a lapis lazuli (a dark blue stone typically seen
in Egyptian-like jewelry) for personal happiness and intu-
ition, as well as opal for mental focus and passion.

I also celebrate the Goddess on every full moon and
at every point on the "Wheel of the Year" (October 31,
Samhain; December 20, Winter Solstice; February 2, Imbolc;
March 20, Vernal Equinox; May 1, Beltane; June 23, Summer
Solstice; August 1, Lammas; and September 21, Autumnal

Equinox). Sometimes I celebrate with a group of like-minded individuals and we drum, converse, and hold rituals. Sometimes it is in private where I dance, meditate, and create art of all types to honor Her. The following is a poem I wrote to Her during one of my celebrations on the full moon:

WITHIN AND WITHOUT
Without Her—
only madness
and footfalls
on broken branches
heard by predators.

Within Her—
soft cushions
of red river womb
and rebirth
of self.
Room to grow in.
And the turning of seasons
to the drumming
of a thousand tribes.

Without Her—
puddles of darkness
drink in the daylight.
And I am falling
without walls.

Within Her—
moon dancing
to the spiral song
of truth.
Of nature.
And radiance drips from
Her tender hips
onto a bed of time.

Without Her
I am lost in
the ebb and flow
of deception.
Within Her
I am held safe
close to her breast
where all life began.

I try to live my life, each day, in constant worship and communion with the Goddess. I try to meditate each day and
live the way I feel She wants me to live—as a loving, hum-
ble, creative, productive, caring, nonjudgmental, helpful,
"good" person. I will not pretend that this is an easy task.
Like any other faith, mine takes effort and dedication, but I
truly feel Her there with me, supporting me. I think that is
why I never felt comfortable in Christianity; I didn't feel a
nurturing force that helped me in my daily life.

My beliefs play a major role in what I plan on doing when I get out of college as well. I have created a career goal that is based soul-ly on my spirituality. I plan to get a job at a museum and work my way up until I have the ability to create my own exhibit of ancient Goddess artifacts. I feel that it is very important for our society to realize that a female power was worshiped by ancient civilizations. Her essence still lives in well-crafted relics from places all around the world, including Egypt, India, and Britain. They are excellent learning tools and should be organized in such a way as to educate people in what they truly were, instead of being spread throughout other exhibits and labeled things like "pagan god statuette."

I also plan on writing literature for people to enjoy, which will have Goddess-oriented undertones. In fact, I am currently working on my first novel, which features a Goddess as a main character. As well as writing, I want to create more art for the pagan community to enjoy. Right now, I am working on creating altars (sacred space areas) for myself and my friends. For now, I do them for free. My friends just pay for the materials and I will paint, tile, mosaic, etc., the designs that they want. However, someday I want to create these altars by consignment, allowing others to enjoy the gift that I was given by employing me to make beautiful, functional pieces of art.

Spirituality is the biggest part of my life, and it affects everything that I do. I have grown inside of the

Goddess and have found my true self and my true beliefs.
I feel that everything that has happened in my life has led
me in this direction. It has all been a learning experience
set forth by Her so that I could come to Her on my own.

Everyone's personal spiritual beliefs are sacred, and
whatever you believe is what you need to survive. A mentor of mine once said that all religions are paths up the
same mountain. I truly believe that. I know that the Divine
has presented itself to me in the form of the Goddess
because that is what I need to live my life. I am proud of
what I believe in, and I am glad that I have finally found a
home nestled in the lap of the Great Mother.

*Pamela Dawn deForest is a writer, artist, priestess, wife, Tarot
reader, herbalist, healer, student, teacher, and lover of all the Great
Goddess has created. A graduate of the University of Redlands
(Johnston Center), she is currently working on her first novel and lives
in southern California with her husband and her two cats.*

Influences of mine . . .

One book: *The Moon Under Her Feet*, by Clysta Kinstler,
because it is one of the only books that I have found that
deals with a real story (that of Mary Magdalene) and incorporates a Goddess myth. It is both stirring and sacred.

One album: Any album by Dead Can Dance, because they
create the most moving, trancelike, beautiful music I know.

One spiritual leader: Joan of Arc. She is, to me, the epitome of a person guided by the Divine.

One artist: Susan Seddon Boulet. When I first saw her work (paintings of Goddesses and totems) I almost wept.

One thinker: Sappho. She is an ancient Greek poet who is one of the deepest yet simple poets I have ever read. And I think poets are the greatest "thinkers" of all time.

About the Art

Untitled, 1996, Oil on Canvas, 20″ × 24″
Gwyneth Tripp, artist

*T*his image emerged for me from between the lines of an academic paper on spirituality in East Africa. The words conveyed a profound spiritual expression, but in order for me to fully appreciate the experiences beneath the writing, I needed to explore them through painting. For me, this image is about intimacy and protection and about finding home.

Gwyneth Tripp *graduated from the University of California, Berkeley, in 1999 with a degree in history. She currently lives in Oakland, California, and devotes much of her time to painting. She has been involved with the Interfaith Youth Core, an international interfaith movement, since its inception. She writes: "The future looks bright though undefined—painting, graduate school and travel—only time shall guide their order."*

Gwyneth began painting as a child through watercolor technique that emphasized color, balance, and cohesion within the small pages used in elementary school. Her paintings have grown larger and her concepts have taken greater shape, but those elements of color, balance, and cohesion remain constant challenges in her work, both esthetically and contextually. In the last few years, Gwyneth's choice of subject matter and technique has moved from direct social commentary to more abstract representations of human form and tenderness, to a combination of the two.

Influences of mine . . .

One book: Woman on the Edge of Time, by Marge Piercy

One album: Red, Hot and Cool, various artists

One spiritual leader: Malcolm X

One artist: Brett Cook-Dizney

One thinker: Cornel West

5

Spirituality vs. Religion, or Why the Atheist Crossed the Road

IAN GIATTI

*R*eligion is a promise. Religion is a demographic. Religion is a battle cry, a nonprofit organization, a ghost from a time less complicated. Religion is a bully, a referee, and a crybaby. It is all of these things. But it is not my spirituality.

It is a matter of obligation now, like family picnics and 9-to-5 jobs. I was born a Catholic-Jew, or a Jewish-Catholic, depending on which one of my parents you believe. My allegedly Jewish mother remained attached in guilt to her mom's half of the family, who were almost all victims of the Holocaust, another bloody crusade in the name of religion. Though her mother was a practicing Jew, I recall many a Hanukkah when I would have to refresh her memory of the Eight Nights. She had never been inside a temple or synagogue; I was more Jewish than she was, if you counted all of the bar and bat mitzvahs I attended in my adolescence.

Her idea of celebrating Judaism was matzoh ball soup and a plastic menorah that usually got blown out by accident. Yes, she made her attempts, but these were attempts at reconciling the tragedy of her family's past with her own secular lifestyle. She had lived an essentially non-Jewish life, and she had betrayed her mother's family in the process. For my mother, Judaism was a memorial, not a religion, and certainly not a practice of spirituality.

My father, the Catholic, was even more detached from his religious birthright. I would ask him incessantly to explain again the difference between Catholicism and Christianity. His answer?

"They're just more fanatic about their Jesus."

He hated churches. Now maybe that had more to do with the connotations of marriage (and the despair of his own) that drove him to this disdain. The only time my dad ever spoke of Jesus Christ was in a letter I once happened upon, one that certainly wasn't meant for my eyes. In it, he recounted a dream in which he was walking around a majestic waterfall fountain encased in shiny, brilliant marble. Looking at his surroundings, he noticed everyone was naked and completely content. There was no strife, no suffering—only tranquility and love. As he splashed the cool fountain water on his face, he heard a deep, rumbling voice that bellowed, "There is no Jesus Christ." He fell to his knees sobbing, because, he wrote, he had known it all along.

So much for Catholicism.

I have never glimpsed it in the rituals, the lighting of candles, the bowing of our heads. Perhaps that is why I am frightened of such actions. I'm afraid they're all in vain, like trying to eat once and for all. These ceremonies are not solutions, nor are they helpful hints. Because ultimately, in the long line of age-old tradition, these rituals do not change. They are amended, yes; shortened and updated for the attention-deficient and the religious contemporary (read: spiritually lazy).

EMPTY RELIGION

But, in reality, these practices feel alien and utterly empty. They are static events in a world that is increasingly mobile and always evolving. Rituals like Communion, for all its inspirational symbolism, have not transformed in a way that authentically reflects the transformation intended for its participants. It has remained practically the same ceremony it was almost two thousand years ago, yet it is supposed to convey the true essence of Christ to teenage boys bred on Playstation 2 and digital music—elements that were nothing less than completely alien when the First Communion transpired. How can Orthodox Jews expect their children to understand the miraculous wonder behind the Eight Nights of Hanukkah? Through chocolate Gelt and little blue lights around the front porch? For most of my generation, these stories have taken their place on the fairy tale shelf, alongside Aesop's fables and Old Mother Goose. They are fascinating, for certain; but where do they fit within the context of our twenty-first-century lives?

I have lost the use of these stories. Their impact has been dampened by the hysteria of adolescence, when I was a proud atheist, if any of those exist. My argument against the existence of God was, of course, the easy one: if we are blessed by something higher, why do bad things happen? Back then, among worrisome acne and low self-esteem, the answer was clear: *We are not blessed. We just are.* It seemed simple enough, a self-contained solution. There was no great meaning or greater force behind what happened to us and who we were in this world. Just bigger ants in a bigger colony, slowly killing ourselves.

I was seventeen. It never occurred to me that life and all its mysteries and surprises were ever beyond the realm of explanation. I would declare to my parents, "There is no God!" over buttered pasta and sourdough rolls on a weekly basis. They didn't seem to mind my blasphemy, as if the same thoughts had occurred to them, and like their thoughts, mine would soon dissipate into a numbed acceptance. And they did, but not until after I graduated from high school, before I first tasted the fruits of true spirituality.

I like to think of depression as a bad, tasteless joke. You stumble, slip, and fall into loneliness, your sense of reality challenged, and you laugh in fear of all the silence.

And just when you think you've got a hold of yourself, just when you think the punchline's coming, the joke replays in your head over and over; you may forget about it for a while, but you can never completely forget it.

We've all heard about the alcoholic who finds Jesus, or the ex-convict who becomes a member of the Nation of Islam. It seems that we feel the need to find some other meaning in our lives only when the one we have doesn't make sense anymore. Our situations demand a strength, an understanding that we don't otherwise possess. So we turn, twisting and writhing with pain, to find our spirituality. My turn was during my first two years away at school. I used to call it a bout with insomnia, but I know now that it was simply depression.

College, at first exhilarating in its freedom, had become less about motion and more about rote movement, academically and personally. My insides felt corroded, drained out. I was lost, awash in a flurry of whys and how comes. School didn't feel normal any more, and my friends seemed altogether less friendly. Anxiety attacks were routine whether I was studying, in class, at a party, or simply trying to sleep. What made everything worse was the feeling that no one could understand what I was going through. Yes, my parents tried—so many toll calls and care packages—but it wasn't enough.

One of those countless sleepless nights, I stepped out on the stairwell outside our dormitory. It was almost 4 A.M. on a Monday, and the whole world seemed still.

Looking out on Goleta, California, I felt like the only person in the world. And it was one of the most terrifying sensations I've ever experienced.

From that point on, I began to understand that I had become a stranger to myself. I had stuffed so much garbage into my life that I was further away from myself than I had ever been. And unlike the past, Mommy and Daddy were not going to be able to make it all better. It was going to have to happen inside me.

So a funny thing happened. I began paying attention. I paid attention to the people around me, the world around me, life around me. But most of all, I paid attention to myself. I would listen to my thoughts and not judge them or interpret them, but simply acknowledge their presence. I watched movies alone, because I wanted the experiences to be mine and mine only. I didn't want anyone's reactions to interfere. I hugged my sister more. I let my mom talk longer to me on the phone because I couldn't tell her that just hearing her voice made my eyes well up. I would jot down lyrics to a song if they made me feel a certain way, and I'd recite them over to myself all day long. I began to read poetry and found that there were people, across the universe and ages ago, who had felt the way I did, saw things the way I saw them. I looked people in the eye more often, my eyes aching to look inside their souls.

I found more God in the eyes of a human being than I ever found at Christmas dinners or Torah readings.

The strangest part is that once you notice, you become addicted to noticing more and more. You don't ever want to take your eyes off the world. Awareness was stirring within me, and it wasn't under the auspices of a church or a synagogue or rules or tradition or the Names of Things with Capital Letters. It was because I was paying attention.

They ask me how. They ask me how I can call myself a spiritual being without any "official" affiliation. But it is precisely because I am bound to nothing that I have been able to rediscover my true essence. By stepping back from my world, and just listening to my inner voice—or "observing self," as Arthur Dikeman called it—I am able to better understand myself. In doing so, the world is a place that I can swallow; it becomes an answer that isn't so elusive. There is no policy, no rigid process that promises a higher state of being—just the incessant longing to become closer to my own being and those around me.

Inasmuch as I have found my spirituality outside the confines of religion, it is safe to say my moral character has been molded with even less religious influence. As far as ethics are concerned, spirituality is really the only genuine moral measurement we possess in the new millennium. The notion of our religious leaders as our moral compass has been antiquated by televangelism, Jim Bakker, and other Christian "superiors" who have tainted young America's respect for all religions. If the last eight years have confirmed anything, it is that our political leaders cannot and will not be held responsible for our virtues as a nation. Scandal and entertainment media have simultaneously proliferated and undermined the ethical influences of celebrities, movie stars, and professional athletes. In fact, even the one sanctuary where generations before have sought moral direction—the family unit—has since been dissolved and redefined. Divorce is now the rule, not the exception, and adultery is accepted merely as bad decision making. As television's children, we were not afforded the same types of moral examples as previous generations.

So, we turn inside. We manufacture a spirituality based on personal experience and subjective belief, and with it we inform our own morality. This leads to a whole slew of problems. Yes, we now have a certain control over our ethical future, where we must make decisions based on our own beliefs and values and not those imposed upon us by an external source.

We are now held accountable only to ourselves and to our own value system, and that idea scares a lot of people. Where it once was seen as mystical and eccentric, personal spirituality now is ostensibly self-serving and utterly flexible. Baby boomers reared on Communion and bar mitzvah understandably have problems with this. But those who practice this new type of spirituality are acting under no pretense but their own impulses. They are honest, not in order to adhere to some ancient commandment but because it *feels right*.

FINDING SPIRITUALITY IN NEW PLACES

I refuse to believe that my intuitive feelings, the sensations I have about God and the universe, can be entirely wrong. Misinformed, maybe; incomplete, perhaps; always changing, certainly. Shouldn't all of our hearts feel this way? Isn't a longing for completeness what wakes us up every day? Isn't our grand, silly search for truth why we breathe in the first place? In fact, it is the isolation we all feel in our own personal journeys that has brought generations of humankind together, to provide a sense of communal search and understanding through religion.

Conversely, Generation Y (Why?) has largely turned away from organized religious communities to help define our identities. Instead, we are searching for ourselves intellectually. In college and university we are exposed to schools of thought spanning the ages and the globe. I can't think of a day when I haven't incorporated some teaching I learned in my Indian philosophy class. Somehow, the two Bible classes I have taken seemed less applicable—more a proponent of folklore than of spiritual growth. Instead, as a declared non-Buddhist, I find that Buddha helps me out every now and then.

There is spirituality in this.

We are searching for ourselves culturally—an inevitable evolution from the Anglocentric upbringings of our baby-boomer parents, whose soul-searching was limited to only different shades of white. The population boom in the southern United States and the ever-expanding diversity of California have restored the notion of America as a melting pot. Our movies and music are created and pulsate with the blood of different races and ethnicities. Women and African Americans, most recently, are now occupants in high government and big business more than ever before.

There is spirituality in this.

And now, we are searching for ourselves digitally, with infinite amounts of information literally at our command. Digging through endless volumes of humanity on the Internet, downloading pieces of our social fabric, our generation and especially the children after us are being brought together at a staggeringly exponential rate.

There is spirituality in this. There is a certain truth in the commonality of being. It is a truth that ancient tribal organizations, the origins of institutional religion, cannot dispute, regardless of their authority.

It troubles me to hear that the elders of this country are concerned for its youth. Yes, this kind of generational grumbling has been going on for as long as I can remember. The fact of the matter is that the only people concerned are those in the religious right, and those whose social and economic status relies on the preservation of institutional religion. If these people were concerned with our truly "finding" whatever it is we are supposed to be looking for on Sundays and in prayer, then our efforts should be encouraged.

In a highly controversial interview, Governor Jesse Ventura of Minnesota said that religion is a crutch for weak-minded people. Although there are obvious problems with this statement, I believe that what Governor Ventura was attacking was not the validity of each individual religion, but the spiritual insecurities of contemporary America. Confronted as we are with a dizzying array of ethnic and religious backgrounds on a daily basis, being a truly spiritual American today is a difficult task. It demands real soul searching and a firm grasp of what we do and do not believe in. But instead of undertaking this task, I believe most of us, both under and over the age of twenty-five, rely on preexisting ideology in our family traditions to guide us down our path. It is the spiritual equivalent of entering the family business. It certainly has its virtues, as any effort to preserve family is virtuous. But are we learning about ourselves?

Is religion helping to define our place in the universe, or is it simply limiting it? Are the immutable Bible or Torah or Qur'an authentic representations of our spiritual identities as human beings?

Religion is not a crutch for the weak-minded. It is merely spirituality in its simplest, most rudimentary form. We have witnessed the hypocrisy, the moral and spiritual mediocrity of succumbing to tradition for tradition's sake. In an age when there are books on everything for dummies, my generation has instead opted to find out for themselves. I am a *new adult*, with decisions to make about my identity and my future. I am not about to surrender this newfound privilege. I am content with discovering my spiritual self through my own avenues. I am not in need of a crossing guard.

Ian Gatti *is twenty-three years old and a creative writing/english senior at California State University, Northridge. An aspiring actor/writer/director, Ian has been involved with the film and television industry since he was six years old. Besides having leading and supporting roles in feature films and prime-time TV series, he has also written, directed, and/or starred in several student films. His passions including reading and writing poetry, playing basketball, and the cinema. But, just as with everyone else, his daily struggle is for the essence of spirituality: not only what it means to live, but to live well.*

Influences of mine . . .

One book: The *Autobiography of* Malcolm X. The portrayal of that rare person whose courage, flaws, conviction, and ultimately compassion gave birth to the stuff of legends.

One album: OK *Computer,* by Radiohead. Finally, an album where the presence of lyrics isn't even necessary: the music tells the story. But this story happens to have some of the most relevant, subversive lyrics to date.

One spiritual leader: J. Krishnamurti. The antithesis to Western ideals about how success is perceived. His "Right Livelihood" will forever guide me through my personal and professional struggles.

One artist: William Blake. From his disdain for organized religion and thought, Blake created his own universe, his own symbolism through the raw power of language in his poetry and vivid, brilliant colors in his paintings.

One thinker: Gore Vidal. Admittedly, I have only limited familiarity with Vidal's works. But his cautious pessimism toward American government and its inner workings carries a sort of undeniable rightness about them.

About the Art

Untitled, 1999, Oil on Canvas, 72″ × 48″
Gwyneth Tripp, artist

*T*he image for this painting came to me as I neared the end of my university education. It is a reflection on being at the edge of something powerful but completely unknown—feeling innocent, curious, strong, and cautious about what one might step into.

For more on Gwyneth Tripp, see pp. 32–34.

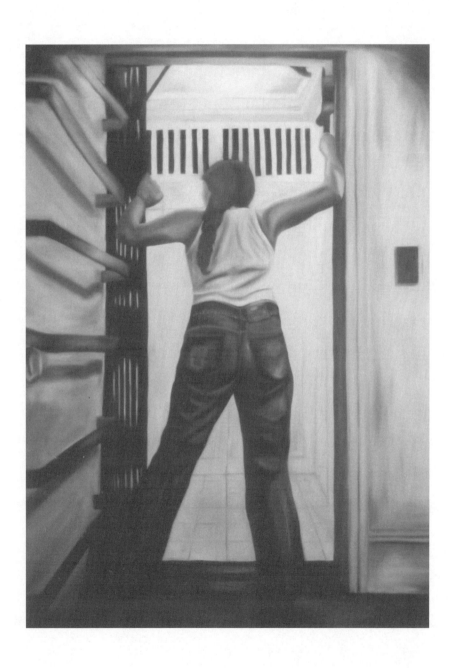

6

A Spiritual Orphan

ARLENE HELDERMAN

*L*ike most people, I have had drastic decisions to make, terrifying tensions to confront, and failing friendships to either end or begin again. But the most overwhelming of them all has been found in fears about faith, the realm of religion, and my sense of spirituality. Because my mother and I nearly died during my birth, everything goes back to this beginning. Just as middle-aged men and women might wake up one day to cancer or heart disease and are shaken out of their self-centered worlds to rethink the meaning of life, I was given this gift at an early age. Out of near-death came great life, and I had no choice but to believe in something sacred beyond my own experience.

Despite our medical miracle, my parents chose not to baptize me and to let me find my own way. I became a naturally curious questioner. Some of my earliest memories are of trying to figure out faith because I felt such a spiritual sense within. Childhood brought Baptist Bible camp, Lutheran religious released-time classes, and several Sunday schools. Later I set out on a spiritual search of sorts— studying various traditions despite my undeveloped intellect, striking up conversations with church leaders, and attending worship with anyone kind enough to offer. Religion was rarely discussed in my family, and yet I inherited an insatiable longing to make meaning out of everything I encountered. I often felt like a spiritual orphan, left alone to answer life's great questions, wandering the world in search of something, not knowing where I was headed or whether I'd ever get there. Fortunately, at seventeen, I began to find my answers in baptism and confirmation into the Roman Catholic Church and through studying theology as an undergraduate.

So I write as a woman who was given an almost unfathomable gift of life over death and who seeks to make sense of that gift. I write as a woman who was raised without religion and who studies theology in the hope of creating companionship throughout her journey. And I write as a woman who converted to Catholicism five years ago, but who now questions that conversion. I question it because I often wonder whether I was so tired of being alone, of being a spiritual orphan, that I simply leaped at the easiest opportunity to belong. But then again, why does anyone join a faith tradition? Why does anyone seek to make sense of the senseless? Why does anyone want to become a part of something greater than themselves?

We all find solace in the spirit of community, and when we are welcomed, we will keep coming back. We all long to play a part in some story, and in so doing, we are drawn out of ourselves in a life-sustaining way that reveals hidden humanity. This discovery is what we live for. Madeleine L'Engle writes: "Why does anybody tell a story? It does indeed have something to do with faith, faith that the universe has meaning, that our little human lives are not irrelevant, that what we choose or say or do matters, matters cosmically."

I also question my conversion because sometimes the doctrines feel overwhelming and faith seems far away. Like other young believers/seekers, I struggle in having a personal relationship with Jesus Christ, in understanding the seven sacraments, and in finding my way in such a pluralistic society. But I have attempted to continue the conversation of conversion through traditional spiritual disciplines practiced in a somewhat nontraditional way. Such disciplines include prayer, study, service, and people.

PRAYER

Maybe I have been left out of some secret that all spiritual people share, but I have absolutely no idea how to pray. I do not want to offer self-absorbed requests and requirements, but I cannot focus only on others at all times. I do not know whether I am to utter lines from famous saints or succumb to whatever words arise in me. I do not know how to be present, how to praise the Lord, or how to keep communion. Can you be taught such things? Is there really any one way to pray? I doubt there is. But I will never forget the inspiring lines spoken by the great Christian writer C. S. Lewis: "If I stopped praying, I think I'd stop living. I pray because I can't help myself. I pray because the need flows out of me all the time, waking and sleeping. It doesn't change God. It changes me." The first time I read this, all I could think was "Wow." I was not sure whether there was anything that I felt so strongly about.

But then I thought some more. And I realized that the way Lewis felt about prayer is the way I feel about writing. I write because I can't help myself, because the need flows out of me, and because I do not think I would be alive in the fullest sense if I did not do that which I so love. When I write, I catch glimpses of self, other, and something sacred. Such glimpses are not just a gift from God but also a gift back to God in the only way I know how to pray. Annie Dillard asks, "Why are we reading if not in hope that the writer will magnify and dramatize our days, will illuminate and inspire us with wisdom, courage, and the possibility of meaningfulness, and will press upon our minds the deepest mysteries, so we may feel again their majesty and power?" Because writing is about meaning-making, it is essential to my spirituality. My writing, my practice of prayer, is an attempt to create what Dillard deems "beauty laid bare, life heightened and its deepest mystery probed."

STUDY

In her masterpiece *Their Eyes Were Watching God*, Zora Neale Hurston writes: "There are years that ask questions and years that answer." Like most lives, mine has been filled with age-old yet ever-present tensions and questions. And like Hurston and her heroine, Janie Mae Crawford, I am a young woman on a search for self and God, asking cathartic questions and believing wholeheartedly in eschatological answers.

When I came to college, I chose theology as my major for two reasons. First, because it best fit an interest sparked long ago. If theology, as Anselm claimed, is "faith seeking understanding," then I have been at it my entire life, for I have always had some spirituality-seeking sense. Second, and perhaps most importantly, because theology is all about questions it is therefore instrumental to cultivating spirituality. I have studied so much within this discipline—from the history of Christianity to Judaism, Hinduism, Buddhism, and Islam. I have dialogued to the best of my ability with St. Augustine, Thomas Merton, Oscar Romero, and Dorothy Day. I have scrutinized scripture, struggled with Christology, and fallen in love with the Kingdom of God. And I have applied to five graduate programs in the hope of one day teaching theology to anxious young students. The study of theology has been a wonderful way for me to integrate questions of spirituality in my life. I have learned so much—and yet, there is so much more to learn.

I believe that we are called to live these years that ask questions in anticipation of a year that has not yet answered. The answers will come at some other time in some other way. Life is obviously too short a time to give us all the answers to all the questions, but it is long enough to let us try. And it's in the trying that I truly live.

SERVICE

Service is an important part of my spirituality. I have discovered through several service projects that I am deeply interested in the way "God talk" enters "street work." Writing and theology are not enough for me, and I long to do something more. That something more has come through work with the homeless and through other activities. I have come to believe that the time to work toward the realm of God is now. That is what I am trying to do.

The first time I ever encountered homelessness, unemployment, addiction, abuse, and environmental degradation, I was overwhelmed by the world in which we live, and I didn't know where to begin. I have found, however, that there is a mutual relationship between spirituality and service. You can't have one without the other. While a sense of spirituality is often the reason we want to work toward a better world, it is also our spiritual roots and resources that sustain us in such work. If we and God work together in this world for peace and justice, perhaps there is hope for humanity. In my own life, I like to think that God needs me, but I also know that I need God.

PEOPLE

Catholicism is concerned with sacraments and many people are surprised that there are seven. As I questioned my own baptism and confirmation, I have many questions about sacraments. For example, I don't understand the exclusive sacrament of holy orders in my tradition. Also, my studies about early Christianity and the historical Jesus have left me sometimes skeptical about the role of reconciliation and the centrality of the Eucharist in Catholic life. And I just don't think much about the sacraments of marriage and anointing of the sick.

I hope to someday deeply believe in the sacraments, but until I do, I must turn to those signs of this world that resonate with me the most. There are sacraments in my life, but they are often offered through ordinary and extraordinary human beings. I previously spoke of my parents raising me without religion, abandoning me to my modest musings, making me an orphan of spirituality. This is not entirely true. When I watch my father walk in the woods, when my mother embraces me, when I listen to my sister sing, and when I am surrounded by the people who know and love me the most, my spirituality is suddenly sacra-mentalized, I find God in the midst of my world, and I am no longer alone. Spiritual sacraments are at our disposal at all times—through those with whom we are close and those we have never known. Therefore, we must learn to take an honest and heartfelt look at the world through the eyes of the suffering homeless stranger on the street, and we must also notice the grace of our own immediate families for the first time. After all, it is these revelations that alter our lives, the way all good sacraments should.

So, what does all of this mean?

We live in a world where consumerism controls, where power is privileged more than service, where weapons seem more sacred than words. It is no wonder today that many young people are skeptical about religion, faith, and spirituality. As Douglas Coupland points out in his novel *Life After God*, many people have the modern mental-ity that they are beyond God. Lots of us don't even want to accept help from our next-door neighbor, let alone from an ethereal existence that lives in another world. We are orphans of spirituality because none of the old illusions will work for us anymore. Our world is too technologically advanced for us to believe that we cannot control our own destinies, and we continue to stagger on an eschatological edge between hope and heartbreak. How are we to foster faith when reason rules? How are we to imagine the other when we can't get beyond ourselves? And how are we to seek the way the world ought to be in the midst of the way the world is? After asking these questions, I think that I am an awfully lucky individual.

I am lucky because I have managed to find some meaning in a seemingly meaningless world. I am lucky because the memory of my beginning propels me in my search for spirituality. I am lucky because I have at last found some spiritual family—through mothers and mentors, fathers and friends, sisters and strangers. I am sure some people would shudder at hearing me recount my conversion to Catholicism, and I wonder as well whether it is authentic. But whether or not my adherence to tradition is unconditional and complete, whether or not my interpretation of the faith is absolutely accurate, whether or not my spiritual disciplines follow a previous path, I am being converted. For conversion is not just a one-time test; instead, it is a constant and continual creation of a way to be in the world.

In the postscript of her spiritual autobiography, *The Long Loneliness*, Dorothy Day writes that the Catholic Worker movement "just sort of happened." Dorothy and her friends "were just sitting there talking" when people asked for bread, or clothing, or shelter, or, in a greater sense, for a new humanity. She concluded that while it "just happened," it is still going on. This is what conversion means to me. People often ask me to describe my conversion to Catholicism, and I really can't articulate it as well as I would like. For far too long, I had wondered about the world of religion, and maybe I sort of fell into Catholicism the way some people fall into their lifelong careers. My conversion was not some great awakening or all-encompassing epiphany. Instead, it just sort of happened. It happened through falling away from faith and finding the way back, again and again. It happened through encountering the evidence in a seemingly sad way and re-envisioning it in hopes of balance, not burnout. It happened by entering into the place of my pain (disappointment and despair at the world) and turning toward the hope of my heart (my spiritual practices of prayer, study, service, and sacraments through people). And despite all that has happened, it is still going on.

Arlene Helderman is from International Falls, Minnesota. She graduated from St. Norbert College in De Pere, Wisconsin, and is now completing a master's degree in theological studies at Harvard Divinity School in Cambridge, Massachusetts.

Influences of mine . . .

One book: *Their Eyes Were Watching God*, by Zora Neale Hurston.

One album: *Mortal City*, by Dar Williams

One spiritual leader: Dorothy Day

One artist: Charity Helderman (my sister)

One thinker: C. S. Lewis

7

An Unauthorized Autobiography

SUMI LOUNDON

WHO I AM & WHERE I'VE COME FROM

To look at me—a blonde, blue-eyed, American-as-apple-pie girl—you'd think I'm more a "Suzie" than a "Sumi." But to know something of my life, to be Sumi makes perfect sense. I was born in 1975 into a small Soto Zen community in rural New Hampshire. There was nothing conventional, either American or Japanese, about this not-quite-monastic-yet-quite-disciplined place. For one, we played Zen basketball, had t'ai chi every day, lived a sharply anti-materialistic lifestyle, did organic gardening before organic was cool, and carried on long conversations about nonattachment, no-self, and nirvana. In my first years of public school, I discovered that how I was being raised was also strikingly different. None of my first-grade classmates woke up at 5:30 every morning to attend meditation: the warm glow of candles and fragrant incense were the first things to greet me in the day, followed by sessions of chanting in Japanese, hitting bells, and bowing. And I didn't know about Cheerios, grocery stores, or Billy Joel until my mother left the community in 1983, when she took me and my three younger siblings to Connecticut upon separating from my father.

Now thrown into the middle class, I experienced a degree of culture shock. Whereas in the community everything from toys and food to time and space had been shared, I now had unlimited personal choice in what I wanted. I began attending a Christian church, soaked up hours of TV time, and tried to recreate communal life by having sleepovers. Everything Buddhist and disciplined dropped from my life as my mom and dad fought in the courts over custody of their four children. After living with my mom for three years, my younger brother Kai and I went to live with my dad.

In my dad's home, we lived a nearly monastic lifestyle of three—plus one roommate and a stray cat that adopted us. My brother and I woke up at five every morning to do hatha yoga and *pranayama* before going to school. When we got home, we took care of the cooking, cleaning, finances, and shopping while my dad tried to catch up professionally from all the years lost in community. Continuing in the unconventional manner of vigorous self-improvement from the community, my dad also spent hours teaching us not only about algorithms, recursion, and other fascinating concepts in computer programming (his night classes) but also about Boolean algebra, calculus (in the sixth grade!), anatomy, indoor golf, plumbing, time and motion efficiency, Socratic philosophy and debate, and hydroponics. Weekends often found us building experimental Buckminster Fuller structures out of pine wood and PVC, or Ralph Glug-glug, our beach-ball and pine wood sailing boat. We had very little money, but my dad's motto, "simple living, high thinking," made us richer than I realized at the time.

My father also had an unconventional take on religion in that he encouraged me to explore as many religions as possible. Mormons and Jehovah's Witness missionaries were not unwelcome when they knocked on our door. Doing Hindu breathing practices and saying grace in Sanskrit in the morning might be followed by studying the Bible in the evening. I was urged to explore readings from Ben Franklin to St. John of the Cross to the *Tao Te Ching*. However, my father was reluctant to express his own belief system because he wanted to let my feet find the path best for me intuitively. The downside of this liberal religious education was that rather than choosing one religion I made a pastiche of practices. I had, to some extent, a case of spiritual indigestion.

It was with this unusual upbringing that I arrived at Williams College, thrown into a situation where, for the first time, I had unparalleled freedom to redefine myself. Like most other freshmen, I wrestled with questions of identity in an intensely reflective way. Was I a scholar or a worker, a good girl or a bad girl, a Buddhist or a Christian, a crunchy type or a business type, one who tried to blend in or one who claimed uniqueness, generally tactful or generally direct, quiet or loud, entertainer or listener, fashionable or unfashionable in a cool way, sex or not sex, drinking or tee-totaler, swearing or clean-cut, fiscally liberal or thrifty? Was my unconventional history interesting, or was it just weird and unrelatable? Would I embrace or distance myself from the events of the past? Trying to answer these questions against such a wide array of ways to live was confusing, at best. If I stuck with Buddhism, then the precept to "refrain from sexual misconduct" could mean it was okay to experiment. If I went closer to the Christian side, then even kissing might be questionable outside a marriage. And as I learned more in the classroom, even religion itself became suspect as a valuable way of living. Perhaps God was just a psychological projection, prayer was just a crutch, religion an opiate.

I temporarily joined the Student Christian Fellowship, since no Buddhist *sangha* existed on campus. To be honest, I was drawn to the Bible studies and prayer groups because of a crush I had on this unbearably handsome sophomore. But I was also drawn to singing in English, to the strength of care within the community, and to the generally well-intentioned spirituality of the group. I began seriously considering becoming Christian, partly because, unlike being Buddhist in America, it was not a constant struggle to explain or to be accepted. At the same time, as

I learned more about what this particular group, InterVarsity Fellowship, stood for (highly conservative views on most things), I felt I could not honestly accept their views. And I felt the precious memories of life in the Buddhist community burbling up: how much I missed the intelligent structure of Buddhism and the way those ideologies played out in the community through tolerance, patience, equanimity, compassion, and wisdom. I could not ignore the seeds planted from those formative years that had now taken root in my mind.

My father gently reminded me, "If you can't find it, found it," and so I started the Williams Meditation Society, which was, while not explicitly Buddhist, a group for similar-minded people. I began to meditate regularly for the first time in years, just watching my mind. The more I watched my incessantly chattering mind and the broil of emotions, the more I became interested in finding some peace and quiet from them. I began to invite dharma teachers from the area to give talks and became earnestly interested in what Buddhism had to say about how one can live. It's ironic to me now that, even with my upbringing, I did not become committed to Buddhist practice until I started meditating, in the very same way that many college students wind up in Buddhism. Perhaps even more stimulating were the questions from beginners, who assumed I knew a lot about Buddhism. I often began by confidently giving answers, only to find myself terribly confused a few minutes later. So I realized that in fact, I knew very little about the history, philosophy, or cultures of Buddhism. I couldn't even say what the Four Noble Truths were!

By my senior year of college, I was so invested in Buddhism that I decided to do a thesis on it. As a fine arts major I did a series of watercolors about being an American and practicing Buddhism, living up to my name's Japanese meaning of "beautiful painting." After graduation, I lived and volunteered at a Theravada-Vipassanā community, taking a year off to reground myself in community and practice. There, in the countryside of old stone walls, I got an inside look at baby-boomer Buddhism as if I were watching what would have happened if my parents had remained Buddhist in their middle-age years. Being in this maturing crowd made me wonder where my peers in Buddhism were.

In the fall of 1998, I moved to Cambridge and started a master's program at Harvard Divinity School in Buddhist studies. Although I had been warned that academic study can suck spirituality out of practice, I plunged in anyway with the faith that my own sense of the sacred would not be destroyed by deconstructing dharma. As it turns out, nitty-gritty details about Buddhism haven't made me lose my faith but instead have allowed me to see that what I believe is contextualized by history and culture. For example, in the 1970s my father used to say that Buddhism is a science, not a religion. I now see that to be more accurate, he should have said, "Buddhism, and mostly Rinzai Zen, can be defined as a 'philosophy' that was introduced to European-American elites in the late 1800s and again in the 1950s to those searching for alternatives to religion and affected by the rise of science, adapted to Victorian sentiments of optimism and activism, and modified by a cultural thread of rugged individualism." The far more complex views of Buddhism allow me to see how I am shaped by—and shaping—culture and history, and how they have given me a much richer sense of the tradition I am part of. Outside the classroom, I have met at last some inspiring young people who practice as well as study Buddhism. Through these friendships, and by meeting young Buddhists from all walks of life, I have become curious about what this next generation has inherited from the baby-boomer Buddhists and what we will claim as unique.

BUDDHISM THROUGH THE EYES OF MY GENERATION

About a year ago I began writing a column for *Tricycle* magazine, reflecting on the younger generation of practitioners in the context of American culture. Being a Buddhist in America is tough work because some of our cultural norms are at cross purposes to practice. For example, we live in a consumer culture aimed at increasing the amount of desire and then satiating it. "Obey your thirst," as Sprite advertises, means that one is subordinate to one's immediate desires. "To be one with everything, you must have one of everything," a car ad proposes, meaning that happiness is a

result of acquisition. Buddhism, on the other hand, advo-
cates reducing possessions so as to reduce desire, and
reducing desire to reduce attachment—the wellspring of
most suffering. I find it very difficult to forgo the permission
to satiate immediate gratifications that consumer culture
gives in favor of simplifying my life.

But a second kind of consumerism has taken hold in
the dharma world—that of spiritual consumption. These
days, books on Buddhism, magazines on Buddhism, cata-
logs for every accouterment to worship and practice, and
spiritual boutiques exist in far greater numbers than in the
1970s, when I first encountered Buddhism. Even in the last
ten years there has been an explosion of supermarket spir-
itualism. Some of the ads for the perfect *zafu* or the best
incense are marketed to already practicing Buddhists, while
other items, like power beads, are so stripped down of their
origin that anyone in the market can "get something out of
it." In and of itself such marketing is not a bad thing, but I
think young people especially get confused by ideas that
"if only I had the right bell" or "if only I had the right statue,
then I would be able to really practice." I've sensed some
vapidness on the part of those who think that one can "get"
Buddhism in a box. Ultimately, the spiritual consumer culture is, I feel, a big distraction.

The second problem I encounter as an American is
that I have an unprecedented amount of access to all faith
traditions. My parents encouraged me to take advantage of
this religious freedom and to explore all the religions and

various sects of Buddhism. What my parents didn't antici-pate, though, was that instead of choosing just one religion and sect and sticking with it, for many years as a teenager I had a strange blend of ideologies and practices. In fusing and confusing Hinduism, Buddhism, and Christianity, I got lost in the range of moralities and practices. And because of this, I had no framework by which to live consistently, eval-uate whether or not I was making spiritual progress, or get consistent community support. It was only when I said, I'm sticking to this practice and this *sangha*, that my practice began to bear any kind of fruit.

Along with freedom comes the freedom to be indi-vidualistic, to construct identity. As individualism has played out in Buddhist America, I meet a good number of young people who have made a Buddhist path that has neither a teacher nor a *sangha*. Some of these paths are quite creative and reflect some trends already begun in the baby-boom generation—such as feminism, opening to the gay community, and democratization—that distinguish convert Buddhism in the West from more traditional forms of Buddhism. On the other hand, I feel some concern that individualism, taken to any greater lengths, might cause distortion and confusion.

The third cultural aspect of the second generation of American Buddhists is that we live in a more Buddhist-friendly society than did the previous generation. What was considered counterculture in the late 1960s and 1970s is now considered hip. Ironically, even though Buddhism today is still considered alternative, the alternative has become somewhat mainstream (like R.E.M., which started out as alternative but became so popular as an alternative band that it kind of took the meaning out of the world *alternative*). My grandparents questioned my parents on everything. They challenged them, asking why choosing to scrub carrots and meditate over professional careers and business suits was wise. Today, my parents are enthusiastic if I take up yoga and decide that I want to attend divinity school. And society at large doesn't roll its eyes when I describe why I choose to be Buddhist.

But one problem that comes with more widespread acceptance is that Buddhism sometimes seems watered down by pop culture. While real estate commercials depicting Buddhist monks expose the public to their beauty, such commercials can also trivialize a sacred thing. Although pop culture can be an expressive tool for young adults in Buddhism, I just hope we don't begin believing that the face value is the whole value in preference to looking deeper.

Although the second-generation *sangha*, my generation, has not matured yet, and it is difficult to find a coherent pattern to identify us, there are some indications that Buddhism is blossoming in the most beautiful way among young adults. It seems that the seeds of sensitivity sown in the 1960s have yielded some remarkable practitioners.

Take, for example, eighteen-year-old Kunga, just graduated from a Milwaukee high school, who recently

ordained as a nun in the Tibetan tradition. She is now practicing in Pema Chödrön's Gampo Abbey, in Cape Breton,
Nova Scotia, and intends to be a monastic for life. How
extraordinary that one so young would trade Gap jeans,
long black hair, a professional career, and a relationship for
burgundy robes, a bald head, poverty, and celibacy!

Clearly, one of the big questions about the future of
Buddhism in the West is what role monasticism will play in
the formation of the American *sangha*. Many baby-boomer
Buddhists play the line between being monastic-like and
lay-like, doing long retreats that are monastic in style but
returning to family and professional lives as lay people. Will
the younger generation continue to blur the line between
monasticism and lay life by integrating the two?

We can also ask what the role of meditation will be
for us. Although the meditative arts are found in all faith traditions, many turn to Buddhism for its highly developed
and systematic approach to meditation. Although in Asian
Buddhism meditation is not emphasized, especially among
lay people, in the West the emphasis is so strong that many
practice Buddhist meditation techniques but would not
label themselves Buddhist. As meditation is often the gate-
way by which many enter the Buddhist path, and as meditation is one of the primary meeting points of interreligious
dialogue, how much further will young Buddhists take meditation in their personal lives and in their communities? Will
the integration of meditation with Western psychology continue to be seen as valuable?

Some say that in addition to the three lineages newly arrived in the West—Theravada, Mahayana, and Vajrayana—a fourth is beginning to take root, that of socially engaged Buddhism. This kind of Buddhism is a small but growing group, bound across lineages and sects, that feel sitting on the cushion is not enough—one must take the fruits of practice into the real world and work for social justice, environmental change, and world peace. Although most of the baby boomers I meet are primarily cushion dwellers, the majority of young adults I encounter are considerably more focused on grassroots activism, seeing inner transformation as more a foundation to engaged Buddhism than as an end in itself. Take, for example, the words of Steve, seventeen at the time I interviewed him: "The way I see it, it's up to us to go on retreat, get regrounded and reenergized, and then jump back into life, where the real teachings are, and experience all the sweetness and brutality . . . and make *that* our practice. . . . I want to become a more effective organizer/activist. Perhaps I'll be able to go to Chiapas, Mexico, and work as an international observer for the Zapatistas." Caitlin similarly views herself as a social justice worker and already, at the age of seventeen, has worked at a queer youth center, on a feminist microradio show, and in an urban garden for children. She hopes to be a community organizer and antiracist activist. In concert with her broad approach, she also plays in an orchestra that uses instruments made of bicycle parts. Jaime, a freshman in college studying environmental engineering, considers as part of her practice being involved with environmental and volunteer groups. Jake, a freshman at Marlboro College studying Burmese language and world studies, would like to aid the establishment of an international force for biodiversity conservation. Perhaps, raised in an ethos of global awareness and a sense of empowerment from the generation before, the next crop of young Buddhists will integrate socially engaged Buddhism into their vocations conscientiously, taking our cues from those before us.

I also see in my generation more of a willingness to be middle class and be Buddhist. In their early twenties, my parents took nonmaterialistic ideals so seriously that they didn't plan for retirement and had no typed resumes. Today, both my parents are trying to catch up professionally for the decades they skipped in favor of an ascetic-like lifestyle. In my early twenties, I feel less idealistic as I buy lipstick for a job interview, have a 401(k), and check out dental plans. The gap between middle-class practicality and ascetic-monastic idealism seems to be closing in my generation, echoed by movements now seen in the baby-boom generation.

Another aspect somewhat unique to this second generation in the dharma is that we now have some who have lived with Buddhism all their lives, who have grown up in a culture of Buddhism in America. Most in the baby-boom generation either flirted or converted or made their own societies. But there are some, like myself, who received a Buddhist vision from their early, formative years. When I run into people like Josh, who is now twenty-eight and was raised at the Rochester Zen Center (of Phillip Kapleau, *Three Pillars of Zen*, fame), we always have a lot to talk about. We can laugh at how awkward it was to be a Buddhist kid because so few of our public school friends understood. For us, for example, living in a community meant significantly less personal freedom and choice than our peers had at home.

I think that those who choose to remain Buddhist from a childhood of Buddhism have a place within young Buddhism at large. We carry the memories of what did and didn't work for the generation before. Perhaps we can serve to remind the young *sangha* that ultimately most of our parents rejected heavy drug use because it furthered escapism rather than a true awakening to the self. Or we can pass on the skillful discernments garnered over time, such as the finer distinctions between detachment and nonattachment, rebirth versus reincarnation. There are very few of these Buddhists around, but I think we can help newcomers feel at ease that Buddhism in America, beyond Asia, has a home here.

And what will be this generation's relationship to the homelands of Buddhism, those cultures in Asia in which Buddhism has flourished for so many centuries? The baby-boomers were the primary importers, but now that Buddhism is mostly imported, will young people continue to make pilgrimages to the East? Will they feel that "authentic" Buddhism can be found only in Asian masters? Will we draw closer to a less-Orientalized picture, or will we huddle in our own groups and form an entirely new Western style of Buddhism? I think that young people will continue to enthusiastically do junior year abroad programs in Asia to study religion. Here's the experience of a student at Hampshire College: "And finally, behind the stupa, Aaron sat beneath the bodhi tree, in the same goddamn spot where the Buddha sat, where the Buddha reached enlightenment. He touched his forehead to the trunk, as he had seen the other pilgrims do, and he felt as if he had come to the center of the world, to the world's origin. And when he finally arose, he was not enlightened but he felt *pretty good*. He felt *okay*."

For a more serious engagement, take, for example, the experience of Teal, a classmate of mine at Williams. Teal started his path by attending meditations as a freshman. Then he went to Japan to find out more about Buddhism. Two years later, he became Suryo-san upon becoming a fully ordained Rinzai monk at Sogenji Monastery in Japan. He now studies environmentalism as intensely as he rises at five every morning before class for meditation.

But do we need to travel so far when in our own backyard, America itself, there exist as many Little Asias as there are cities? One characteristic of the previous generation of Buddhists is that there has been such a gap between the Asian Buddhists and all other Buddhists, who are primarily white middle-class and upper-class folks. I find it ironic that the "white Buddhists" travel so far away to get their dharma when beautiful temples serving primarily ethnic people are right here. Both groups are isolated by language barriers and fear. But there is a tremendous amount to be gained, I think, from cross-cultural dialogue, and I hope my generation will courageously do it.

Perhaps this generation will have some advantages in bridging the gap between Asian Buddhism and Western Buddhism because a good portion of us are of mixed heritage. Take, for example, Shari, a twenty-nine-year-old woman who was raised a Buddhist in the City of Ten Thousand Buddhas. She's half Chinese and half Jewish, and practices a blend of Hua-yen Buddhism and Judaism while working on her Ph.D. in early Chinese religions at Stanford. Because she embodies both American and Chinese cultures, she works to bring together the two communities she travels between, to help them learn from each other. Ones such as Shari, because of their dual heritage, may bring about a closer and more amicable relationship of the two cultural Buddhisms we have in the West.

In my movements as a Buddhist in America, I'm witnessing the graying of my *sangha*. I wonder about how my peers will absorb Buddhism and where they will take it. We will possibly be distinguished from those before us by our stronger call to socially engaged Buddhism, by the closer relationship and dialogue of Asian and Western Buddhisms, and by a kind of pragmatic approach that keeps our feet on the ground and our heads in the clouds. Those who were raised Buddhist can perhaps keep us from making the same mistakes our parents made while retaining clarity of vision. And how we will relate to monastic–lay issues alongside meditation practice may unfold in a very empowering way. We are challenged, however, by the powerful draw of consumerism and by the potentially ungrounding effects of hyperindividuality and freedom to choose. Overall, the second generation—my generation—offers tremendous potential for the unfolding of Buddhism in America.

Sumi Loundon *was born into a small Zen community in rural New Hampshire and lived there for eight years. She has a B.A. in fine arts from Williams College. The author, still a Buddhist, now lives in Cambridge, Massachusetts, where she is a graduate student at the Harvard Divinity School, studying Buddhism and Sanskrit. She is also the editor of* Blue Jean Buddha: Voices of Young Buddhists *(Wisdom Publications).*

Influences of mine . . .

One book: Maura O'Halloran's diary published as *Pure Heart, Enlightened Mind.* It was very important to me to read about a contemporary young woman, my age, who really "got it," and bested all the Zen male monks in Japan. It added a dimension of Buddhism I had never considered, and that was not so evident in reading about that exalted lives of the Buddha, or bodhisattvas, or saints (all male, by the way). She wasn't some old nun up in a remote cave a thousand years ago, but someone I could relate to right here and now. Very inspirational, beautiful, honest.

One album: The Hindu bhajans I learned at an ashram showed me how music can be a powerful spiritual connector. Music is divinity when it's done a certain way.

One spiritual leader: My parents. They certainly had the most religious influence on me, hands down. They taught me meditation, yoga, t'ai chi and introduced me to Hinduism, Christianity, Buddhism, Taoism, Advaita Vedanta, Greek philosophy, and so on.

One artist: Whoever did the Gandharan art, and the art of the area in Afghanistan. These Buddha sculptures are a true East-meets-West confluence: the graceful Hellenic lines in the face, and the symbolism and iconography of India. The art speaks to the two sides of me in ways that other Eastern art does not (seems more remote). The faces are truly serene and lovely, handsome, godlike, and yet very human.

One thinker: Robet Gimello, professor at Harvard University. He has managed to totally overturn my preconceptions about Buddhism, which interestingly enough has had a profound effect on my internal understanding of practicing Buddhism.

About the Art

"At Ease with the Buddha," 1997, watercolor on guache.
Sumi Loundon, artist

For more on Sumi Loundon, see page 77.

8

Jesus H. Christ, or How I Learned to Stop Worrying and Love the Church

EMLYN BEAN

*A*s a child I was sometimes eager to die. I wanted to know what would happen. Death was less a morbid fascination than a great feeling of anticipation, the way I felt when it was the night before my birthday and I thought something really great would happen as soon as I woke up, if I could ever get to sleep. I was not by any means seeking escape from an unhappy childhood. I was just curious. Someone had told me that things actually continued to happen to you after you die. This was tremendously exciting to me. Being an impatient child, I wanted to know what heaven or the afterlife was and what it looked like and felt like. Good thing I never took that curiosity into my own hands. Fortunately, the connection between actually dying and experiencing an afterlife hadn't yet been established in my mind.

Growing Up in Liberal Religion

I was a happy kid, growing up with my parents and my
brother in a brownstone in Brooklyn, New York. My mom is
an American Baptist minister. Tucking me in bed at night,
she would repeat, "The Lord is my shepherd, I shall not
want . . ." and so on. I learned the prayer, I know that much,
I can recite it. So did I enter the kingdom of heaven as a
child? Was that my ticket? What little I had read of the Bible
had led me to believe that childhood was my one chance to
accept the religion that my parents were practicing, to make
it into that big birthday party in the sky.

My curiosity and the prayer were my beginning.
They are where I start.

My spiritual experience began at church, an
American Baptist/United Church of Christ congregation
where mom occasionally preached, a fairly left-wing, artsy
liberal church in downtown New York City. My mother and
father were married there, and my brother and I were raised
in their Sunday school. We didn't learn a whole lot about
the Bible or about Jesus—some, but not much. I knew who
Jesus was. I knew most of the important and quotable Bible
stories. I learned that God was not male or female but was
whomever and whatever God was. Jesus was not a messiah
and not our savior—or if he was, we certainly didn't talk
about him that way. The Good News at my church had more
to do with Joseph Campbell than with Jesus, and since you

can't teach Joseph Campbell to little kids, we didn't get a lot of Good News, just arts and crafts. I learned in Sunday school that Jesus died tragically, but nobody ever got very emotional about it.

Needless to say, our church avoided "Jesus talk," which we considered trite and simplistic—and besides, most adult members of our congregation had come to this church to recover from their Catholic, evangelical, or otherwise dogma-laden upbringings. I was a member of the generation after them, one of their own kids. I wasn't carrying any sort of baggage from a strict Christian upbringing, but I grew up with a lot of very cerebral left-wing theology. While other young Christians across the country were singing, "Jesus wants me for a sunbeam," the kids in our Sunday school were taught the "Garden Song." It was all about planting and weeding, reaping and sowing—not Bible thumping, just nice, nonthreatening gardening. Believe me, I'm not complaining. Considering that I took to wearing black nail polish in the seventh grade, I wouldn't have made a very good sunbeam.

When I was fifteen, a friend offered to take me to a church service for women one Sunday at a huge convention center. I happily agreed, imagining hundreds of feminists all gathered together to talk about God and their issues within the church. Instead, the place was packed with thousands of women who were all there for one reason only: to praise God. I was profoundly uncomfortable. There was a lousy comedian/emcee who introduced different speakers, artists, singers, and preachers. One by one, women came up to be baptized in a huge swimming pool on the stage, shouting their affirmation that they do believe that Jesus Christ died for our sins, that he was the one and only son of God the Father, who is the Lord our God, and undeniably male. Never before had I felt like such an atheist. My beliefs didn't sound like this. My faith was a far cry from that big swimming pool. Deeply troubled, I walked home afterwards, clutching my copy of Joseph Campbell's *The Power of Myth*. And then I remembered a story my mother had told me.

Years before, when she was no more than ten years old, my mom attended a straightlaced congregational church with her family in a lily-white suburb of Chicago. Her family vacationed in the summers in Wisconsin and attended church there as well. It was a hot Sunday one summer, and she was walking home after church with a family friend, an older woman and a wise one with a mouth to match. Down the road, they passed a spirited and raucous revival meeting in a tent: sweaty, scarlet-faced preacher, little cardboard fans, hands raised and tongues unleashed in song and speech, crying "Mercy, mercy, mercy." My mother was quite taken aback. Just as she was craning her neck to look closer at this strange specimen of religiosity, the wise woman walking next to her leaned down and said, "That's your Jesus, too, Holly." Live with it. That Jesus is the swimming pool baptism Jesus, the bumper sticker Jesus. I can hear the same woman saying to me: That's your Jesus, too.

You have inherited a complicated and bloody myth that is reflected in everything from mass-produced "I Love Jesus" t-shirts to the horrors of mass slaughter and genocide in his name. What does it mean to you?

These questions were still lingering inside me when I decided to major in religion in college. I hoped that by knowing more about religion from an academic standpoint, I would be able to understand my feelings and my faith, deal with my conflicts about God and Jesus and the Christian church. I was also (and still am) passionately interested in the history of religions, in different theologies and ways of believing. Little did I know the kinds of responses I would get when I told friends about my major or my religion.

NEEDING FAITH

"I mean, Jesus was a right-on dude, you know, he was it. But this whole monotheistic God thing, I don't know, I just can't get into it." Terry put down his beer and looked unsteadily in my direction. I was feeling ready to leave the party. Despite his less-than-sober state, though, Terry's words caught my attention. He said he had been raised an atheist in a left-wing radical feminist household, not unlike a lot of my friends. As a college student he had examined religion through the lens of anthropology. "I mean, look at the agricultural revolution and the rise of cities, you know," he said, reaching for another cigarette. "Up until then, it was just polytheism—hey, there's God everywhere, in trees and water and air and everyone, you know. But once you get this development, this need for centralized power structures, suddenly there's just one God, no ifs, ands, or buts. How can that not be political, you know?" "Yeah," I murmured, glancing at my watch. "Sometimes I wish I had faith," he said. "And I do, you know. I believe in my brother and my mom and my family. You gotta have something."

Later that night, I sat behind the wheel of my car, staring a bright red stoplight in the face. The streets were empty, inhabited only by sleeping neon and stucco store-fronts. A roadside church bulletin board whined "What's Missing in Ch - - ch? UR!" I couldn't stop thinking about Terry's point of view: it's faith we need, but the church often seems to be built on something other than faith. For many of us in the American college-age set, admitting that you have faith—or worse, that you need to have faith—is a brave thing to tell another person. Discussing religion is one thing, but questions about faith are reserved for times of depression, desperation, or heavy drinking. I constantly wrestle with the Christian church's teachings and its history, but I'll confess: like Terry, I need faith in my life.

My questions about faith arise from either need or curiosity, depending on when you ask me. I often wonder about the nature of perception and how it affects faith. For instance, what does it mean when your eyes are just sight, just a sense—like hearing, smell, or taste—and then there comes into your being a presence, a knowledge of the world beyond sense? Some people spend their lives trying and trying to enter that world, to stay there for more than a few seconds at a time. People say it's golden there; people say it's God there. I want to know how it moves us beyond ourselves. I want to know how the unseen shapes our lives, how perception is the thinnest, thinnest veil over this world of the unseen. I am seeking the soul of the world, I say to myself. I am asking to be transformed.

But this is curiosity. This is not need. I have some idea of what need feels like, too. It's when the wrecking ball is about to hit and no God I know is going to stop it, and no person I know has the power. When human beings destroy each other wantonly and with little or no remorse, in the name of money, power, and even God, where is God then? Some of us need to believe in order to survive; some of us need to believe that God is not anger or judgment but only love.

And that God is available to us.

To each her own. Needing God is not so easily classifiable. People need God because they need answers. People need the hand that holds the future, the book in which our lives are written. People need God because they need to be forgiven for the things that no human being can forgive. People need God because death does not make sense—has not ever made sense—at a very basic level, to any human being. Death proves us wrong on every count. The universe, the Great Life and Death Machine, is too vast to exist in my mind without God. Terry said it: You gotta have something.

SOMETIMES FAITH HAPPENS

My own faith happens when I'm not watching. It guides the actions I take in the world when I'm not thinking about them. It often embarrasses me, since I can't account for it intellectually. Accepting my faith means relinquishing control over myself, and this attack on the ego makes the experience of spiritual change especially violent. My brain has a hard time letting go, but when it does, faith often makes itself known to me by means of a swift kick to the gut that I call grace. It reminds me none too gently that I've been changed, whether or not I'm aware of it.

One of these violent experiences of grace happened to me recently, in the midst of my extended process of leaving home. Each time I return home from college, I find that home moves on and changes without me. My church, which is part of my home, part of my known geography both spiritually and physically, is changing. It is undergoing an enormous renovation, a process of death and rebirth. The house and the garden adjacent to the church are being torn down partly because the church can't afford the renovations necessary to keep them up. The house and garden both have a long and glorious history; they hosted many artists, thinkers, preachers, runaways, drug addicts, servants of the church, servants of the city and of God. The history of this place includes me as well. My growing-up place is old and decrepit and needs either a miraculous makeover or a peaceful death. So we held a predemolition wake for the place. The churchgoers, my second family, came to the garden to make little memorials from what bits of earth and trash and memories they could find. The destruction of this building and garden was an event that I hardly thought about until I walked through those familiar rooms and realized that they would be blown away, so much dust in a matter of days. It was too much. The thought of losing that physical part of my spiritual home was a thought that came down hard and heavy on me.

The garden that night was a mess of tiny altars. The condemned house loomed above it, wheezing, muttering, crumbling, as proud as it was old. I was reminded of my grandmother in her bed in Illinois just two years earlier. Grandma was propped up on a dozen pillows, and the eight or ten or twelve of us kids and grandkids were hushed in her room, holding her hands and feet, touching whatever inch of Grandma we could reach, and listening, listening to the soft in and out of the last breaths she took. Where was she headed? In those moments I was fully aware of things: the sun, the curtains moving, the specks on the wall, the blue walls, the smell, the feel of things in one room at one time in one tiny, tiny place in the whole universe. I was fully alive in that room, even as my grandmother was giving up her claim to life. No one can ever know when she gave it up and when it was taken from her. A split second, a movement of two forces: one known, the other nameless. Death, among other things, is an unfathomable mystery to me.

Death is constant, and death changes nothing. But in that
moment, the moment when her final spark suddenly disappeared, what forces were at work there? Who was pulling
the strings? That moment was my first glimpse into the
workings of a universe churning into itself, day in and day
out, making new and extinguishing old. My childhood
curiosity about death was abruptly reawakened, and it des-
perately wanted to go back to sleep. I was terrified.

Although this place we were eulogizing was not a living breathing person, it was a sweet old monument full of
memories, full of history. It was a place. The people in our
congregation couldn't stop telling stories about the old
house and the garden and all the crazy and beautiful and
worshipful and blasphemous things that went on there. All
I could remember were the people who had watched over
me in that house and the very first thoughts I had begun to
have about God just fifteen or so years ago. I was just plain
sad to see the place go, and the stupid sentimental sadness overwhelmed me, flowed into me like blood from a
wound that wouldn't clot. Maybe I was also crying for
Grandma, for anyone I had ever known who had died. That
moment of extinguishing life was opening up again, a hungry old world revealing itself. Stunned, astonished, and
bewildered, all I wanted was for someone to say to me, "Just
give it up to God, honey. All that sadness, let God take it."
But no one would have said that to me, not there. How sentimental that would have been, how overwrought, how out
of fashion for our hip little downtown church.

On the way home in the car, the blood still wasn't clotting. I couldn't stop crying. My mother said softly, "I bet you've never really heard the Gospel preached to you." She was right. I had never imagined it would be something I would want to hear, much less need to hear. My church had raised me to believe that the Gospel wasn't necessarily full of hallelujahs and exuberant hymn singing. The Gospel I learned at church appealed to my head, sometimes to my heart, but rarely to my spirit. I had never known it any other way. I had always liked the fact that my church got me thinking and had raised me to be a hard-nosed critic of popular culture, of conformity, of the Christian church. But none of that really mattered then. Something like death was just a little too present right then, and it wouldn't go away. It was a powerful kind of hurting, and it opened up a place in me that just needed a little hallelujah, a little Pentecostal rise-up-singing. My mother the minister just said to me, "You know what the Gospel is? Here it is: you're forgiven. Not by me or by anyone else, but by God." In that place of irrational spiritual need, where I needed soothing, I understood. No, it doesn't make sense—I didn't want forgiveness right then. I wanted to be reminded of the presence of God, and for some reason it was suddenly apparent to me that God had been there all the time.

I had been changed by my need for faith. My need had become my faith. I won't apologize for it. Call me sentimental, but I think I may be a Christian. God help me.

Emlyn Bean *is a senior at Vassar College, majoring in religion with a minor in music. When she's not singing, sitting in meetings, planning events, making puppets, listening to music, reading, or writing papers, she likes to eat and sleep.*

Influences of mine . . .

One book: Holy the Firm, by Annie Dillard

One album: 99.9 Farenheit Degrees, by Suzanne Vega

One spiritual leader: How about two? Will Campbell and Thich Nhat Hanh

One artist: Peter Schumann of Vermont's Bread and Puppet Theater

One thinker: Madeleine L'Engle

9

Oy, Estherla

*O*n Purim when I was a child, my Hebrew school class put on skits of the story of Esther. Besides the fact that I was one of the first girls to volunteer each year, I was often chosen to play the lead role because my Hebrew name was Esther Malca: "Queen Esther." I was designated a queen at birth, and during these sloppy, usually awful, and always poorly acted skits, I was regal on the *bima* in front of my congregation, giggling through my lines.

After my bat mitzvah, however, I felt dethroned. My bat mitzvah was the turning point in my Jewish life as a woman, but not because it was the traditional Jewish coming-of-age ceremony or because it was held on April 29, 1989—exactly my thirteenth birthday. After that night, I was no longer welcome on my Conservadox (combination of Conservative and Orthodox) synagogue's *bima*. I could no longer play a leadership role in my religion. Junior Congregation, with its skits and fun, ended abruptly, and I was thrown into the main sanctuary to sit with my parents. The tunes were different, few participants seemed to smile at all, and the women were present only in chairs on the main floor.

Currently, at the age of twenty-four, I find myself again at the throes of a lifecycle ceremony. This time it's a self-imposed and nontraditional one that does not possess a name or rituals. Simply, I'm trying to determine what feels spiritual to me about Judaism and find a way to successfully incorporate this spirituality into my life. I am trying to feel proud about being Jewish, even when at times I find myself religiously sidelined for being a woman.

Having never attended a yeshiva or pursued an advanced degree in feminism or theology, I feel woefully inept at properly articulating my Jewish experience. I simply lack the language.

What I can offer is a basic, gut-level analogy: It has been like coming face to face with a brick wall.

Conservadox Judaism led me down an easy-to-follow path for thirteen years, and then it deposited me in front of a brick wall, abruptly ending my journey. For eleven years I have stood and stared at this wall, engaging in an inner battle: Why did I need to reach this wall in my spiritual journey? Why have I found it impossible to conquer this roadblock by myself?

Until this year, when I physically uprooted and resettled myself in the heart of a lively and progressive Boston Jewish community, I was stagnant. I felt as though I had reached the end of the possibilities Judaism offered me as a woman. Even now, with alternatives in my midst, I am finding it difficult to shirk the traditions that have been ingrained in my Jewish consciousness. Though I wish to proceed forward in my Jewish learning, before I can, I must first redefine what I've been told my entire life is the "right way" to be Jewish.

At the time of my bat mitzvah I equated going to synagogue, keeping kosher, celebrating holidays, and dating exclusively Jewish males with Judaism's version of spirituality. Therefore, I fell short on finding what I was looking for or needed in Judaism. I greatly enjoyed my all-female youth group activities, summer camp, and talking with friends in the bathroom during services. But these activities were social in result and cause. Even if I found them empowering or if they uplifted my spirit, they couldn't "count." No—spiritual Judaism meant observing laws, following rules, and living by commandments. There could be no freedom or loftiness involved.

What I didn't understand then was that devouring my aunt's cinnamon cheese rolls on holidays, that spreading contagious giggles at the dinner table at camp, and that braiding my dad's *tsitsis* and getting lost in my own thoughts during High Holiday sermons were all Jodi's version of being spiritually Jewish. Laughter, fulfillment, introspection—yes, they all counted. Yes, they were all important. But since no one validated these things for me, I assumed they were peripheral.

During college, when I was pulled away from what was habitual about Judaism—Shabbat dinner, biweekly youth group meetings, a kosher kitchen—I began to feel disconnected from Judaism all together. When I realized that I missed it—even those things I disliked, didn't under- stand, or felt excluded from—I began to question why.

This questioning resurfaced rather unexpectedly in a magazine publishing class in graduate school two years ago. The final project for this class was to create a new mag- azine: design scheme, editorial concept—the whole she- bang. The magazine I conceptualized targeted unaffiliated Jews. It was a glossy, entertainment-driven magazine intended to almost unconsciously encourage its young pro- fessional readers to believe that it's cool to be Jewish. I called it *Kesher* and slapped an old black-and-white picture of Barbra Streisand on the cover. What I didn't realize at the time was that the main reader I was unconsciously trying to encourage was myself.

While researching possible competitors for *Kesher*, I stumbled across JewishFamily.com, an online magazine geared towards helping young Jewish families incorporate Judaism into their daily lives. When I called to ask ques- tions, I found that Jewish Family & Life!, the company that publishes JewishFamily.com, was in the planning stages of creating a new webzine for twenty- and thirty-somethings— a magazine that sounded eerily like *Kesher*. Ironically, the magazine was being conceptualized right outside of Boston, where I was doing my graduate work.

I then became an intern for this new webzine, called GenerationJ.com and, after a year and a half, became editor. Presently I work forty hours a week, cultivating content through which Generation Xers converse and argue with Judaism. My personal search to find meaningful and applicable spiritual aspects of Judaism has become a daily one.

COMING TO TERMS WITH TRADITION

I discovered in middle school that I would not be successful in following all the rules my grandparents were taught to follow in order to be considered good Jews.

For one, I couldn't shake the desire to date goys.

The few boys I dated during middle and high school were tall and blond, not Jewish. I knew in sixth grade, when my first "boyfriend," a skateboarder named Brian, took me to the movies, that my grandparents would not accept my inter-dating. They sat me down for a chat.

"Jodi, you know it is very important to us that we are Jewish. Is it important to you too?"

"Of course, Grandpa."

"Then you want to marry a Jewish boy, right?"

"Yes, Grandpa."

"Then you should date Jewish boys."

I learned early to follow instructions and play by the rules. In return, I got love from my family and A's from teachers. I so badly wanted to do right by my grandparents. From what they said to me, I inferred that my dating habits were destined to bring me pain. If I went by instant attraction or intellectual connection alone, I would hurt my family. If I wished to remain a good Jewish girl, a boy had to be Jewish first if I were to consider dating him at all. My ethical dilemma became one usually reserved for gays and lesbians: why would G-d give me these feelings if I weren't meant to act on them?

In the sixth grade I learned to consider dating a prerequisite for marriage, a resume builder in preparation for the ultimate job. I began to analyze a touch, a word, an action, for meaning. Dinners, movies, and phone conversations were not mere frivolities; they had context. In a sense, I was married off at age eleven.

During my adolescence, my budding womanhood increased my distance from the religious side of Judaism. The possible female role models I had in synagogue were women who wore *sheidels,* made *shittachs* for their friends' children, or shook hands with congregants in recognition of their father's, son's, or brother's excellent job reading Torah.

It felt as though Judaism deemed me unacceptable or second class for qualities over which I had no control— my attractions to men, and my gender. An overachiever in both academics and extracurriculars, I wanted others to shake hands in acknowledgment of my accomplishments.

And though I continued to explore my spirituality with each passing year, the leadership roles I assumed fell outside the synagogue. I became active in B'nai B'rith Girls, eventually becoming our local chapter president and the North Jersey Council vice president. I used social leadership to garner accolades. My parents attended my speeches and promotions, often shaking hands on my behalf. And I felt proud to be Jewish and a leader in my Jewish involvement. I learned from it that I enjoyed writing speeches and participating in philanthropic events. Judaism became a positive cultural part of my life.

When I started college, I went to a Hillel ice cream social but could not relate to the students involved in the organization's activities. It appeared as though they looked to religious observance for spiritual enlightenment and enjoyed socially interacting with others who did likewise.

Though there were Jewish sororities and fraternities, I didn't join the former or mingle regularly with the latter. I wanted diversity and was attracted to difference. I found the homogeneity existing in the mostly Jewish groups to be overwhelmingly banal. I also didn't wish to claim my Jewishness daily. I knew that my religion was an integral part of my culture and personality, and that its possibilities were something I wished to further explore—but in the future, not yet.

At my bat mitzvah I read from a photocopy of a *haftorah*. I was not allowed to hold the Torah with my own hands, and I was not shown that the Torah was my book of guidance as a Jew. The absence of these gestures spoke volumes about the double-edged sword a girl is entrusted

with when she becomes a woman in the eyes of her traditional synagogue; when I was given the rites of passage, it
did not feel as though I had received full and equal rights.

Today, most of my Jewish female peers—even those
with successful professional lives, advanced degrees, and
traditional Jewish backgrounds—do not attend synagogue
regularly or even keep kosher. They don't apply ritual practices to their daily lives. But the one tradition they do follow, to the best of their ability, is a social tradition—they
strive to marry Jewish men.

In my opinion, the popularity of SpeedDating,
online dating sites, and for-profit Jewish singles event plan-
ners are the result of contemporary Jews looking below the
belt to find their "spiritual" connection to Judaism.

The peers I know who attend synagogue semiregu-
larly go to places like B'nai Jeshuran in Manhattan, where
young professionals constitute the majority of the audience. And before these peers get to services, they primp as
if they were going to a bar, which could very well be where
they do go when services are over. It therefore becomes
questionable whether they attend synagogue to make
some form of spiritual connection with God or simply to
make social connections with possible dates.

Perhaps if today's young professional women felt
more included in traditional prayer rituals, they would
attend services for the sheer spirituality of them and
increase the amount of Judaism in their daily lives.

In defense of prayer rituals, however, I will say that it feels as though the tide for women is turning. A prayer group called Women of the Wall recently made big legal strides in Israel when the High Court of Justice instructed the Israeli government to change policy and enable them to pray at the Western Wall, which includes allowing them to wear *tallitot* and read aloud from the Torah.

And, as the generation behind me has started becoming *b'nai mitzvot*, I've likewise noticed a change in their coming-of-age experiences. For example, at my cousin's bat mitzvah in a Conservative synagogue in Orlando last year, some of her peers were wearing *tallitot*. These *tallitot* were purple and pink and had been given to them as bat mitzvah gifts. Congregation members were acknowledging girls as full and equal participants in the service, and they were ceremoniously expressing this hospitality by wrapping the equivalent of a warm hug around their shoulders.

Though otherwise traditionally Conservative, the Orlando synagogue strays from the tradition of prohibiting women from participating in the ceremony. Women read from the Torah and are given *aliyot*. The rabbi officiating at the ceremony talked in his sermon about how Liza's mother had been an integral member of the selection committee that had brought him to become leader of the synagogue. As he went on to tell jokes about Liza's family, it became evident that my cousins were incorporating their synagogue into their daily lives—a synergy with which I was unfamiliar in my own experience. Hopefully, they will not encounter brick walls during their spiritual journeys.

NAVIGATING JUDAISM WITH A FEMALE COMPASS

In Hebrew school I introduced myself as "Esther Malca, but you can call me Esther." No one else had two Hebrew names, and I didn't want to be different. We all joked about our Hebrew names: Whatever, *Shoshana*. Shove it up your ass, *Yaacov*. Outside Hebrew school, the only person to call me Esther was my grandfather, and even then only through song: *Oy, Estherla, Oy, Estherla, Ich Bin, Meshige Far Dir.* ("Oh, Esther, I love you.") Though I occasionally thought it endearing when he sang my name to me, I didn't value it much then, either. My Hebrew name became my second name. A technicality, nothing else.

My lack of Hebrew mastery didn't concern me, even as valedictorian of my Hebrew school class, because I wanted to pray in English. I wanted to feel ownership of the words I uttered, to understand the prayers I flung heavenward. It didn't bother me that my Hebrew school taught its students only enough Hebrew to follow along with prayers. What did concern me, however, was that the boys, with their limited Hebrew knowledge in tow, still received more rights in the eyes of our synagogue than I. Even those who did worse in class.

This gender-based injustice resurfaced when my grandfather passed away two years ago. My mother decided to say Kaddish, the traditional mourners' prayer, for her father, and recited it morning and night for eleven months. Though she had grown up in an Orthodox household and felt compelled to say Kaddish for her father out of a sense of duty, Halachah does not require women to do so.

Therefore, when she stood and prayed in honor of her father, she did not count towards the *minyan*—the ten men needed in order to say the prayer. After my grandfather's funeral, males needed to be culled from neighboring houses and the synagogue's committee in order to fill the *minyan*. I was outraged by the fact that my grandfather's own kin didn't hold as much weight in the eyes of Judaism as did males who had never even met him.

And yet, the irony is that when I try to escape from some of these traditions I find sexist, to try and reform my Jewish experience, I'm overwhelmed or made uncomfortable by what I find. Reform synagogues, for example, even with their great abundance of English and their female participation, still feel unfamiliar and less spiritual to me than Conservative services. I'm used to traditional tunes, to no-clapping and no-organ-playing policies. My cravings for reform conflict with my inherent associations with tradition.

One Simchas Torah when I was young, my childlike quest for inclusion found me marching in the circle along with the boys, carrying a mini-Torah and singing gleefully. I

innocently disregarded the gender roles assigned by
Judaism because I wanted to celebrate the completion of
the yearly Torah reading in the same way my male classmates did. The rabbi, however, was not entertained by my
shirking of tradition and pulled me outside the circle. He
reminded me that I was a girl and that girls don't march with
the Torah on Simchas Torah, which also meant that they
didn't on any other occasion, either.

At the time, I might not have realized the injustice or
the sexism, for I don't remember crying. I imagine I took
comfort in the existence of such traditions, and followed the
rabbi's instructions like a good little girl. I greatly respected
my rabbi, with his warm, large hands and kind eyes, and I
wanted those eyes to look down on me favorably.

This same rabbi praised me in front of my family and
friends at my bat mitzvah. "I've been watching Jodi *daven*,"
he said as he stood next to me on the *bima*, "and I am
impressed by her ability to follow along with the service."

Ever since starting Hebrew school eight years earlier, I had watched the boys learn to blow the shofar, read
directly from the Torah where there are no vowels, and care-
fully wrap *tefillin* around their arms and foreheads. Following
along with the service seemed easy in comparison with
these other things.

As I came of age I began to wonder if that was all
there was to the prayer experience and to synagogues in
general for me as a woman. Though I was eager to participate, it seemed that my sex and the very traditions I fol-

lowed withheld me from the service. I was introduced to the brick wall just as my adult spiritual journey was beginning.

As a young adult, in the Boston suburb of Brookline, I now live close to temples, kosher restaurants, and other Jews, and this has infused me, seemingly instantaneously, into a community. I have tried a few of the popular social events, formed new friendships, and made possible romantic connections. I've seen how location is important in increasing more than just property value—living near other Jews can make it easier for one Jew to be Jewish.

I'm in no way saying that all my insecurities, gripes, and frustrations have disappeared because I moved my belongings across town lines, but sometimes change needs a catalyst.

I have no doubt that when and if I marry a Jewish man, I will become both more religiously and more spiritually Jewish. I'm just unsettled by the reality that even in this new century, one Jewish woman's desire to gain access, no matter how strong, can be unsuccessful simply because she's outside a community's boundaries and single. Without iron resolve, which is difficult to possess as a teenager or young adult, a female can easily fall out of Judaism's grasp.

Following men's examples, it's no wonder that I eventually found myself lost: Men are fundamentally incapable of guiding an experience that falls completely outside of their own patriarchal traditions. And how could I have expected them to? It was women whom I needed as guides—women who were, on the whole, lost themselves.

Like me, they had been thrown into the thick of Judaism with no female compass.

I may never completely understand what has brought me to the wall and to have all these questions. Likewise, I may never be able to propose feasible solutions. But I wish to recognize that as a young, professional, progressive, traditionally raised Jewish woman, it feels that a piece or two is missing here somewhere.

Jodi Werner *is editor of GenerationJ.com and project director of ritualwell.org. A graduate of the M.F.A. creative writing program at Emerson College, Jodi has recently completed her first feature-length screenplay, a romantic comedy. She lives in Boston.*

Influences of mine . . .

One book: *The Sleep-Over Artist,* by Thomas Beller

One album: Guster's *Parachute*

One spiritual leader: Yossi Abramowitz

One artist: Pablo Picasso

One thinker: Anita Diamant

10

Letting Our Spirits Free

JENNIFER A. JOHNSON

A few weeks ago, while working at a high school retreat, I sat and watched as a young girl in the small
group I was leading struggled with spiritual and theological questions. The tears rolled down her face as she worked
her hands together as if they were Play-Doh. Each of the young
people in our small circle was nodding compassionately in
agreement throughout her story. We understood her pain.
When this young girl finished with her story, everyone in the
group turned and looked at me as if to say, "Please heal this
. . . say something reassuring . . . explain to us where God is
when bad things happen."

She had lost her aunt to leukemia and swore to us all
that she would never enter a chapel or a church building again.
She looked at me through her tears and said, "I know there's a
God; I believe that. I'm just really mad at Him."

Last year, I decided to accept a job at a retreat center
near Chicago. As my first career choice after graduating from

college, working with teenagers on retreats has proved to be more fulfilling and more challenging than I had ever imagined. I feel blessed that so many of the young people I work with feel comfortable enough to share their honest feelings about their own spirituality with me. On many retreats we enter into moving discussions that never cease to amaze me. Part of the reason I believe they feel comfortable enough to talk is that I appear young to them, maybe less intimidating than most adults; but I also think that the students I work with are able to sense that my spirituality has been challenged in similar ways as their own spiritual paths have been. The gift of our connection is not that I preach to them a new way of thinking about God but that I am able to sympathize with where they are in their spiritual journeys. Together we create more mature and reassuring images of God and consider how God is somehow present in our lives. My passion is to help these students realize, most importantly, that they are valuable in this life, and second of all, that their curiosity and questions about God should never cease. Only when we give up on the questions have we truly given up on our faith.

SORTING OUT WHAT FEELS DISTANT AND INCOMPREHENSIBLE

When I first started working at the retreat center, I figured that I would have to be full of insights to share. I would let people know that it is possible to live spiritually healthy lives even if you are struggling with your religion. I thought I would be handing them the key to an important secret—a secret about not giving up on God even when you feel as if you want to give up on everything that is supposed to represent God. What I quickly found is that most young people already have this key but simply no lock to put it in. Let me explain.

On one of my retreats I made the mistake of asking a group of Catholic high school juniors what their opinions of the Church were *before* asking them about their images of God. Unfortunately, this prevented good spiritual reflection for the remainder of the retreat. Our discussion was lively, but the students could only focus on the negative aspects of organized religion. They spoke passionately about the ways in which they feel that going to Mass does little or nothing for them. They spoke of the Church's rules that seem outdated and how many of their pastors could not connect with what was really happening in their lives. Also, the rituals were boring and foreign to them. How could they appreciate the long and usually solemn Eucharistic ritual if the words and prayers were unexplained to them? The students told me of religion teachers at their school whose agenda, it seemed, was to turn them into super-moral heroes, and how these teachers would probably never allow the type of venting that was going on in our small group discussion to happen in their classroom. I offered some weak suggestions, such as the *possibility* of there being *some* wisdom behind the rules of the Church, but overall I was a flimsy boat on a rough sea. I left the group feeling a bit disappointed, but it was evident that healing begins simply when you allow people to speak openly and honestly about their spirituality.

Since that retreat I have always made it a point to ask the students what their images for God are before diving into the larger, deeper pools of religious opinions. It's amazing how people's tones change when they are talking about their religion versus when they speak about how they understand God's part in their lives.

I think it is important for each of us to practice the blending of faith and religion. With religion, for example, we find support, organization, and a sense of community in our faith-sharing experiences. But not always, and not for everyone. Many people have not experienced a sense of community in their religious lives. Even more disheartening is that many of the students I work with and many of my peers seem to be searching for that sense of community in other experiences that are far from life-giving. Experiences such as shallow sexual encounters and getting high with the same group of friends over and over again provide a short-term, false sense of belonging and contentment. These types of activities top the list of quick fixes for feeling "loved," and young people are often deceived by them.

It is understandable that these things are what many people turn to in order to find wholeness before they turn to their own spirituality. We live in a society where media controls everything and money will buy anything. Sex and drugs are offered constantly, whereas spirituality is left unexamined, and religious traditions are something distant and incomprehensible to many people, especially to my generation.

We have also grown up in a time when our parents and grandparents stressed to us the importance of attending religious services (for me, it was Mass on Sundays) but couldn't quite explain to us why going was so important. We are a generation whose faiths are not saturated in fear, as it seems our parents' youthful faith may have been. Instead, our faith is our choice, and the passing on of religious tradition is a gift that we are not sure we want or need to unwrap.

I believe that a religious tradition is a gift worth exploring, but how do I explain that to my friends who feel that this unidentifiable gift has been forced upon them? There is a beautiful sense of mystery when we speak about the way God exists in our lives, but we easily become frustrated when trying to reconnect our faith to our more ambiguous religious traditions. The desire and the natural ability to be spiritual beings is present (the key), but the venue in which people can safely express and adore that spirituality is missing (the lock).

LOVING WHAT RELIGION REALLY MEANS

For part of my college career, I attended the College of St. Benedict in Minnesota. There I met a Benedictine sister who became a friend and a gracious teacher. One night she invited me to join her community for their nightly prayers. Afterward, she and I walked around the beautiful church building where she herself had taken vows, years before I was even born. She explained why the structure of the building was built as it was and showed me pictures of what the chapel looked like when she was my age. Our time together seemed magical, yet the stories we shared with each other were very real. We sat for a long time in the church with only each other and the moonlight streaming through the windows as she told me what it used to be like to attend Mass. She described the amazing moments of holiness that she had experienced through rituals that someone my age might consider to be old-fashioned and crazy, but she also filled me in on her favorite spitball area in the chapel. That evening I learned more about the beauty behind tradition than any class or book could have taught me. I saw the delicate importance in her face as she described why this building and this community had created so much life within her. When I left her that evening, I knew that I still longed for family life more than I could ever long for religious life, but I also knew that I would be missing out on the complete understanding of the wholeness that she had found in religious life. Her gentle words and inviting questions gave me a gift of understanding that I wish my friends could also be blessed with.

I am convinced that now, more than ever, young people are attempting to grab onto something, anything, that might help our spirits feel alive. When I think back to that great conversation with my Benedictine mentor, I remember how evident it was that she had attained a sense of wholeness through her religious practice and faith community. I also had the opportunity to have her in one of my theology classes in college, and I saw how she was still able to ask questions about God (just as the students I work with do) that seemed to enrich her spirituality rather than take from it. The journey toward her theological and faith-filled beliefs was created through a balance of experiences and education. From there she was able to appreciate the mystery of theology and to grow in faith with the loving support of a community and continuous involvement in a tradition. I believe it would have been much more difficult to grasp onto a healthy faith community and tradition if she hadn't first been able to confidently develop beliefs within herself.

My generation is trying to understand religious traditions that seem foreign to our experiences and that become even more confusing given the little religious education many of us have had. I believe that many of the religious rituals that exist, Catholic or not, can indeed be connected to and beneficial for young people's faith lives. But there are those missing links between spirituality and religious traditions that cause so many of us to feel disconnected. I am grateful for the theological education that I had during high school and college. Learning and study have been important pieces of my own spiritual development.

My faith, my appreciation for the mystery, and questions surrounding God are grounded in a growing foundation of understanding. I am grateful not only for a better understanding of the complexity of scripture but also for the opportunity to be awakened to the beauty of other religious traditions and different ideas about God. However, there is so much more to know, and the acceptance that it is okay to struggle with and question our own religious tradition and others is always important. But perhaps most important is committing to our faith quests; if we do that, I think we find the key to bringing spirituality and religion together.

THE BEAUTY OF OUR SPIRITUALITY

There is such a thing as unhealthy spirituality. We are a generation in search of acceptance and love, and it seems that we will go anywhere to find it. Many times, I think, poor resources and a lack of unconditional love at home and school can lead young people to hold on to anything that is going to offer them comfort, acceptance, and "love." This includes, for many, drugs, sex, and gangs, but I can also see how easily my generation can be pulled into extremist religious groups for many of the same reasons. I have met many young people who have turned to these groups after living what they deem an "immoral" lifestyle. This often means that they become more filled with judgment of others than with life-giving, loving habits. Their minds become closed to the possibility of growth and change. They cling to the sense of community and self-forgiveness often found in a "conversion" experience, but unfortunately they seem unable to forgive those who do not follow the rules and regulations given in their religious groups.

We in Generation Y did not create the society that often tells us what to think and feel, and that sometimes seems to offer so few options in life and spirituality. We did not create religious traditions that often feel blind or angry and harsh. We landed in what feels very much like hard reality. But nevertheless, the possibility of finding healing and renewal in spirituality is possible in religion. I want my peers to see that.

I believe it is possible to bridge the gap between spirituality and religion and create the Kingdom of God here and now. Religion is not something that can be forced on a person in hopes that the person will appreciate it someday. Instead, those of us involved in religion should explain and show why we are attracted to our traditions and rituals, and why we believe that faith is something worth exploring. We must show people that they are loved and respected. It is not enough to assume that the people we love know that they are loved by us. Only through kind actions and words that tell of our love will true love be realized. Even though it may sound too simple, if a person doesn't feel loved (young and old alike), nothing else seems to matter.

The people I meet are bursting with inspiration. Their spiritualities are beautiful, but according to most young people, not many adults truly notice their beauty. It is easy to forget that behind the face of every child, teenager, or young adult there is already a story forming that deserves attention and respect. I think that if we worked more on loving and listening to each other across many generations, the rest would fall into place. With open hearts and open minds it is possible to unlock the connection between spirituality and religion, and only then will the spirits of my generation be free.

Jennifer A. Johnson is from Green Bay, Wisconsin. She grew up in a family of five children (she has four brothers) and graduated from St. Norbert College with a major in theology and a minor in peace and justice studies. She is the winner of many awards for public service. Her career ambitions include working with inner-city children, teaching theology on a high school level, and public speaking on the topic of merging spirituality and sexuality.

Influences of mine . . .

One book: To the Lighthouse, by Virginia Woolf. I can still remember the rooms of the house and the complexity of life that each character so honestly exhibited.

One album: After a long day I like to lie on my floor with my journal, a candle or two, and Sarah McLachlan playing in the background.

One spiritual leader: My uncle, Terry Nelson-Johnson, has had the greatest effect on my spiritual life. He has given me the knowledge of what it means to be loved in order to give love.

One artist: The first time I visited the Chicago Art Institute, I could not tear myself away from Monet's pictures. My wonder of what each of his characters were wondering is what pulled me in.

One thinker: Dr. Paul Wadell, associate professor in the religious studies department, St. Norbert College, De Pere, Wisconsin: my teacher and role model. Dr. Wadell is a great theologian and has taught me how to think with my mind and heart in balance.

About the Art

"Cat Sit," 1997, watercolor on guache.
Sumi Loundon, artist

For more on Sumi Loundon, see page 77.

11

Moving from Judaism toward Christ, and the Christians Who Tried to Stop Me

LAUREN WINNER

riday night, I felt very conspicuous. Walking home from the library, I was stopped at a street corner by a Don't Walk sign. Next to me stood a trio of girls, all sporting knee-length black skirts, black tights, and shiny black loafers with heels. They all had broad smiles, sparkling earrings, and shiny dark hair styled in sophisticated coiffures. That I was decked out in a wrinkled flannel shirt and my hair was knotted carelessly at the back of my neck didn't bother me. I felt conspicuous because I was carrying a purse.

Usually, carrying a purse isn't noteworthy. The streets of Manhattan, after all, are filled with many purse-carrying twenty-somethings. But on Friday nights, in my neighborhood, many women don't carry purses, because many women in my neighborhood are Orthodox Jews. Orthodox Jews are bound by laws called *muktze*, laws that govern what you can and cannot carry on the Sabbath. You can carry anything you are allowed to use: a spoon, a shirt, a Popsicle, a book, a ribbon. But you cannot carry a candle, or a vial of ink, or a dollar bill, or car keys, or a pen, or scissors, since writing, spending, driving, kindling a flame, and cutting are all activities forbidden on Shabbat. And there is another caveat. You cannot carry anything, even a spoon, from a place that's private to a place that's public. You cannot carry a spoon from your house to synagogue, or back again, or even from your kitchen to the kitchen of your next-door neighbor. Only around your living room, into your breakfast nook, into the bathroom, into the den—but not out onto the street.

I knew the three women on the street corner were Orthodox Jews not only because they were purseless. There were other clues—clues that told me not just that they were Orthodox, but where they fit on the spectrum of Orthodoxy, a spectrum that runs from exactingly strict to daringly lax. These girls were the latter. Their skirts just barely crested the bottoms of their kneecaps, meeting the strict modesty code but still remaining stylish. Despite some rabbis' opinions that putting on makeup during the Sabbath is forbidden, these three were all wearing fresh dark lipstick. Their shortish skirt lengths and their puckered pouts told me these women were "In the Fold" but liked to push at the boundaries. They would earn frowns of disapproval in synagogue the next morning from their stricter coreligionists, whose ankles would be covered by long dresses and whose faces would be washed clean.

Most New Yorkers don't recognize all these clues. Sartorial subtleties like skirt length are things only an insider would know. But then, I was an insider. The last time I lived in this neighborhood, two years ago, I was an Orthodox Jew. Then came twenty months in England. When I moved back to Morningside Heights, it was as a Christian. I was changed, but the neighborhood wasn't. Everyone I knew in college was an Orthodox Jew, save for a friend from Maine, a friend from Alabama, and a professor or two. Maine had moved to Brooklyn and Alabama to Tennessee, but my Orthodox friends were still in the neighborhood. They still prayed three times a day, waited six hours between eating meat and milk, and danced whirling, drunken, sex-segregated dances at their weddings.

As it happened, I did not know the trio on the corner. I would guess they are sophomores who came to Columbia after I left. They did not have any idea, as we stood waiting for the light to change, that I knew they were probably heading to East Campus, the dorm where the coolest members of Columbia's Orthodox community gather late on Friday nights, after redolent Shabbat dinners, to drink soda and wine and eat Stella D'oro cookies and sing Shabbat songs. We crossed campus together, and, without thinking, I began to hum a Sabbath tune. One girl turned around and stared.

I was not baptized until I moved to England, but Jesus had been tugging at my long, modest skirts well before that. As a teenager I had been fascinated with

Christianity, and in my freshman year of college I signed up for a New Testament class and sat for hours in the medieval art room of the Metropolitan Museum. What kept me interested in Christianity was something very basic: the idea that God lowered himself and became a man so that we could relate to him better. In Christianity, God got to be both distant and transcendent (the Father part), and present and eminent (the Son part—I wasn't so clear on the Ghost). Christians, unlike Jews, spent their time talking to a God who knew what it was like to get hungry, to go swimming, to be tempted.

It was the logical culmination of anthropomorphism—of assigning God human characteristics. All through the Torah, God is pictured as having hands, a face. The rabbis say that of course God doesn't really have a hand, but the Torah uses the language of faces and hands and eyes so that we will have an easier time wrapping our minds around this infinite, handless God. That God would then become an actual man to help us understand him even more appealed to both the novel-reader and the theologian in me.

Though the idea of God-made-man was fascinating, I didn't believe it was true. The rabbis had said the messiah would do certain things, Jesus hadn't accomplished them, and that was that. But gradually Jesus wormed his way into my life, never mind what the rabbis said. In the middle of college, I had a dream and woke up convinced the dream had come from God and the dream was about Jesus. The summer before my senior year I read a novel about evangelical Episcopalians—and then reread it, and reread it again, three times in a single week—and felt sure I wanted what those fictional characters had. Also, I felt sure that in that dream, as in the fascination with medieval Christian art, God had been telling me where to find it.

The Christians I knew, though, didn't seem to agree. After returning to campus after that novel-reading week, I attended a lecture where an Episcopal priest told the audience that Jesus was our cultural expression of the divine truth that all people lust after, just as Kali was the Hindus' cultural expression. During the Q&A, I raised my hand. "Probably I missed something," I said, "but if Jesus is just our cultural expression of a universal divine impulse, why do we say the creed?" The creed, explained the priest, is our culture's vocabulary for giving voice to divinity.

I called a Presbyterian minister I had known casually since I had been a freshman. We met at a local pastry shop, and I drank cider that scalded my tongue as I told him I thought I was beginning to believe in Jesus. Scott's response was that I was Jewish, and I should stay Jewish. "You can't just divorce Judaism," he said, urging me to make an appointment with the campus rabbi. Later Scott said to me, "I had no idea when you told me you wanted to get together that you wanted to talk about Christianity. I thought maybe you were going to come out to me as a lesbian"—a coming out that, in this era of identity politics, probably would have been more acceptable to him than a Jewish student talking about Jesus Christ.

It took God sending me to England before I found a community of Christians who actually believed anything. Just as well: I don't think I had the personal fortitude to do anything more than flirt with Christianity in this neighborhood, where my entire identity was bound up in Orthodox Judaism. It has been trying enough to move back, Christian identity established, and explain to people who knew me in that earlier dispensation why I'm in class on Rosh Hashanah, why I wear sleeveless tops, why I eat at non-kosher restaurants, and why a small silver cross hangs around my neck. Even my professors, understandably, look uncomfortable, and weakly hazard, "Didn't you used to date a guy who wore a yarmulke?'"

But I have found that Jews are not the only ones who ask questions. Scads of my evangelical Christian acquaintances have said to me, "Don't you regret all that time you spent studying the Talmud? All those hours poured into making sure your kitchen was kosher? All the teeth you broke trying to master biblical Hebrew?"

The professors' questions are much more reasonable than the Christians' questions. To put it plainly: no, I don't regret a minute spent over the Talmud, piecing together rabbinic minutiae about dietary laws; nor do I regret the time spent implementing those laws in my kitchen.

Scott spoke with prescience when he said I couldn't divorce Judaism. The first time I ate non-kosher food my senior year of college—it was a bowl of clam chowder—I felt as if I were filing for divorce. It was the only metaphor I could come up with. Once I entered the church, I fled from all things Jewish. I traded my Hebrew siddur for a Book of Common Prayer and sold all my Jewish texts to a used bookstore in Chapel Hill, donated my *havdalah* set and one of my *tallisim* to a synagogue. I gorged on lobster and drank the driest, most expensive bottles of Amarone I could find. The only Jewish habit I couldn't give up was baking challah, which I kept at every Friday: two, misshapen braided loaves, made with whole wheat flour from the recipe my friend Latifa taught me when I was thirteen.

But Scott was right; I couldn't divorce. I am as bound to Judaism as my parents are to each other. They aren't married any more, but they have two daughters together, so they still talk, still see each other at graduations and weddings, still see the other's eyes and nose in their daughters' faces. I find myself forgetting the rabbis' words and needing them, so I am reconstituting my library and trying to put myself back together. Judaism has conditioned everything. It has conditioned how I read Scripture, and how I pray, and who I think Jesus is.

This is not to say that my understanding of Jesus and my reading of the Bible are somehow better than those of Christians who don't know the first thing about Judaism. But I do think the church could stand to learn a few things from Judaism—starting, perhaps, with a deep knowledge of the Torah. I would go so far as to say we have a lot to learn from some of the rabbinic commentary on the Torah, too, but I'd settle for a sermon every now and again that acknowledges the Bible doesn't start with Matthew. Or consider the Sabbath. I would never advocate that Christians embrace the curious and confining laws of *muktze*: Jesus knew whereof he spoke when he talked about the burden of the law. But for all its legalism, the Jewish Sabbath—a time utterly set apart from the six days of work that precede it—seems more in line with what God meant when he told us to honor the Sabbath and keep it holy than dashing from church to the mall. Or to a soccer game. Or to a conference call. And Christians in non-Christian universities—or at least the Christians at my university, starting with me—have something to learn from the Orthodox Jews at Columbia. Within days of my freshman orientation, all my professors, hallmates, and fellow middle-school tutors knew I was an Orthodox Jew, because of the skirt and the dietary restrictions if nothing else. I wonder, with some shame, how many of my fellow first-year grad students know that I am a Christian.

Lauren Winner *lives in New York, where she studies* U.S. *history at Columbia University and worships at All Angels Church. She is a frequent contributor to* Christianity Today, Books and Culture: A Christian Review, *and the* Christian Century.

Influences of mine . . .

One book: I *Could Tell You Stories,* by Patricia Hampl

One album: The Jussi Bjorling and Victoria de los Angeles recording of *La Boheme*

One spiritual leader: Rabbi Haym Soloveitchik and Father Henri Nouwen

One artist: Sculptor Karl Bitters

One thinker: Terry Eagleton

12

The Journey to the Alligator Juniper

SHANA LANZETTA

The journey begins . . .
    Create
Cherish the moment,
    the solitude.
Be the strength like
    all else.
For they need yours
    and you need theirs.
    Love that.
Accompany the soul of
    life on a journey in
        destiny, beyond
    time, through space
        and into reality.
Laugh at evil and
    Embrace goodness.

Happiness is found within
All—through all, and
outside
   of nothing.
The intangible is the most
   comprehendible.
Open to that thought,
   and to that love.

I was sitting by a stream in a secluded place in the middle of town with my philosophy and religion class. My assignment was to find a place of my own and to write something in my journal. I forget what. But what I realized in that solitary moment was the connectedness of all life. This was to become the beginning principle in which I created my belief systems of the world, my place in it, and my God.

BECOME ALL

200 years old—
   she speaks.
she tells me she
   is watching.
   and it hurts.
she gives me a hug,
   an embrace.
   i cherish it.
she is beautiful.
   she is beauty.

she belongs to me.
    and i to her.
    beyond comprehension
we love each other.

behind, above, beyond
    Her—he speaks.
he is a child, yet ancient.
    he tells me a story.
a fable, perhaps
    but maybe
real life.
    he is monstrous
    but so gentle
and intangible.
i like the comfort.
    the solitude.
i understand him
    and he i.

We are one but
    do not touch.
i told him i would listen.

below Him a sound
    calls me—
outreaching and out-
    stretching infinity.

i am longing for that peace,
    that strength, that
glory that she gives me.
beware of interpreting,
    it is dangerous.
almost a mistake
    for maybe
the secret to all
    is not knowing.
her call beckons me.

She is lifted and tugged by
him.
    he is my friend
    and my enemy.
he is my sound.
he tells me the
    story of life, creation,
    eternity.
and i smile
    for I know
    we will meet again.

In my struggle to relate what I believed to be true about the world, I found myself alone, lonely and in need of someone who felt as I did. In this world we seem to be guiding ourselves with the wrong type of compass, and sometimes, even though we know that we are misleading ourselves, we

have no choice but to stray from our path. How we return
and if we return is what really then seems to matter.

the rain fell and i cried.
the rain cried
and the lord cried.

in an open field i walked.
the flowers and grass
played with my feet.
the sun shimmered into the meadow
creating monumental rays upon the earth.
the robin sang and the squirrel jumped.
peace was in all
but me.

the lord came down to me in
the form of a sparrow
colored yellow and green.
the lord sang to me,
"why is it that you are not at peace?"
what has disrupted the flow?"

"i do not know," i wept.
"please forgive me."
then the lord left me.
so I fell to the ground and
cried in anguish.

the lord heard my cry
    and once again came down to me
    this time as a dragonfly.
the lord whispered to me,
    "why do you weep with such passion?"
i could not answer.
       and so i wept more intensely.
then the lord sang,
    "child of life, peace is beautiful.
all that is here possesses that beauty.
    and you, yourself, do too.
place the earth in your hand.
    does it hurt?"
       i shook my head.
    "do you believe it possesses life?"
    i smiled yes.
"then know that the earth-ground-mother
is at peace with you.
    hear the sound of the silent.
listen to all that you cannot perceive.
know the difference between
    what you see and hear
and what you take into your being.
all the love starts from you,
      for you cannot accept
    another's love if you yourself
      have none to offer."

then the lord god held my hand
>as an angel of mercy
and walked me to a stream.
the stream protested in bubbles and laughed
>at the fish.
at once i heard the silent agreement
>>of peace, of unanimous consolation
and again i began to weep.
>the lord smiled and questioned me.
>>"why is it that you cry now?"
and the lord knew. the lord
knew i wept for joy
>that is found in peace.

Sometimes finding god is a struggle. Other times not. Sometimes it seems as though we know that god is there, alive, strong, and present. But yet, we cannot seem to find the answers. Perhaps it is not that god is not speaking to us. Perhaps it is that we are not listening to the silence from which god speaks to us.

SHADOWS

I hear her voice, the voice of the weeping willow.
>I long to hear her words:
>draping sounds of sorrow—
>I cannot help but weep.

I do not weep from sadness or sorrow
But rather from all of the

       joy I see through the eyes of the sad.
           I weep for the peace and happiness I find
           in her.

Her wisdom of the breadth and wind of life
      has been pulled into her roots.
She is beauty beheld in a single form.
She created the wonder of the simplistic.
I ask her, "Please wrap your heart around me
      and take me into your shade."

       Her reply has no words
           but I can hear her response all the same.
       She tells me a story:
           One of faith and courage.
       I ask her where the love is.
           She tells me with a smile
           it comes from the soul.
       Faith and courage can only come
       with love.

And so I leave her to step into the light
      Knowing there is always shade
        Under the weeping willow tree.

I heard this once and have never faltered in believing the
sincerity of this statement: you must die many deaths to
live. I have died many times. But always I am reborn.
Sometimes the death is painless. Other times it feels that

you are bleeding yourself to death. But there are those great moments of rebirth when you begin to see why you are constantly dying. Why you are always killing yourself. You begin to see yourself not as yourself, and suddenly, for a brief existence, you begin to believe in yourself. Sometimes that's all you need.

There is a moment in time
        When you feel the outer recesses
        Of your soul break
        And you feel that you are breaking
        And that you have lost yourself.
But in that same moment you
        See that this is really not so
        But that actually you are coming
        To understand the greatness and
        Wonder of your own being
And although you wish you could
        Offer a sigh of relief in that moment
        You are too awestruck and blinded
        By your beauty that you
        Become speechless.
And for a moment, you think you have
        Lost that opening to your soul
        And you want to cry and scream
        And hold onto it with all your might.
And you try. And soon you lose feeling
        In the hands that grasp so desperately on the door.

And you feel light-headed and dismayed
Because you feel you have failed.
But what you don't realize is that
You haven't failed but rather
You've found.
And in finding you must let go.
Let go of old habits, images and
Ways of knowing yourself.
You begin to see yourself as others
See you and your eyes are
Widened in atrocity
Because what you see is so beautiful
To your heart that you feel you have
Betrayed yourself by lying for all
These years.
So then I say to you—let go.
Open the door to your soul
And let the world in, for it
Is a beautiful and wonderful place.

Living a life that honors the sacred and that truly feels the
world as beautiful, I often find it hard to feel settled in a
world where most of my peers are skeptics and nonbeliev-
ers. It is not that they do not wish to believe; they just can't
seem to. Not yet. Many times I have felt hopelessness at my
place in this world. I have felt alone and restless, and I have
felt confused by my own duality. Do I follow the world or my
own heart? Should not the two be one and the same? Yes,

of course. But they aren't, and I feel as if I might drown if I follow the crowd, but I feel as if I might starve from loneliness if I take that road less traveled by. It's a struggle I am just now coming to terms with.

> like a tornado crashing
> through the stillness
> swirling wind and violent
> sand thrashes about the air.
> dust is thick and visibility low
> the damage is done.

> then the still peace arrives
> the clear air and vibrant sky
> the silence is calming and the sun is
> beautiful.

> there is a path of destruction.
> clearly marked territory beside
> the sacred beauty of the land.

> you are like the earth
> giving bountiful nourishment
> strong, plentiful and rejuvenating
> your strength and purpose
> divinely brought.
> comforting whispers of silence made
> giving birth to all that is beautiful.

> thank you for this life.

My struggles are twofold. One is the struggle of living a spiritual life that always seems in need of company. The other is living a spiritual life as a woman and in need of a voice. I think that perhaps, for me, the struggle to find my own feminine spirituality has brought me the most confusion and heartache. My desire for my own individuality and womanly strength has been crippled by my over-giving and nurturing sides. It seemed that I was always losing this battle. But one day it hit me like a flash of sunshine through a broken cloud. I knew what I saw, and I had no choice but to believe it. I also realized that I had a guiding and living force in the palm of my hands and never thought to look there.

THE WOMAN I SEE
I once met this woman
Whose innocence was a strength
Until one day it made her blind.
She suffered pain
She cried
She fought
She tried.

She came to learn that battles
are for the weak
and knowledge for the strong.

Her face changed.
Her body changed.

Her heart changed.
     Then one day she
     became Alive.
Alive as the tree that
     gives life to the spider
that feeds the bird
that colors the sky with song.

She cried for joy
She wept in pain

She understood that the only
     perfect life worth living
          was one wrought with imperfections

She is looking at me now
confused and enamored.

Some days I awake expecting
     to see her face
Other days I think she
     has found a new home.

Then there are those most
     extraordinary days where she
     appears from the darkness
     wrapped in light.
The light of womanly im-perfection.

I wonder when she'll stop
   looking at me staring back
at her in that glass plate?

For all the things you have taught me
My worth has meant the most.

In retrospect, I look back at my short life and realize how far
I have come to get where I am now, only to find that I am
right where I started. It does not surprise me: the idea of life
moving in circles, engulfing what it needs to survive, then
realizing that it really does not need such a big circle and
that it does not need all this excess baggage. Or care for
most of it. And then I finally realized that my wants and my
needs were exactly the same, instead of thinking that they
always had to be different. God is good to us. God is many
things and is all around. My god is not your god. And for
good reason. For without variety, what a stale place we
would be. My only hope is that you have a god, a good and
glorious god. For without one (or many), I fear for our future.

EVERGREEN EYES
The cool water calls.
   it beckons.
Its beauty is overwhelming
   the clear, crisp, evergreen movements believe
   Each new direction of flow
   brings a new light, a new way,
   and a new thought.
The water's depths are infinite.

If you look close enough
>   The universe entire is revealed
>   And the stars, planets and the black
>   Space is engulfing—
It becomes just as warm and comforting
>   as the water.
>   They are one and the same.
I believe in the water—the cascading
>   monuments of life.
>   I cannot help but open my eyes
and smile.
>   And smile.

Someone once told me of a river
>   that wound around a monstrous
>   mountain covered in deep, strong
>   standing trees.
Each leaf of every tree knew the presence
>   of the other, as well as the surrounding
>   water
>   In harmony they co-exist.
>   but as one in the same side of life
>   and death.
This river overflowed with life.
>   In each drop the essence of knowledge
came forth.
>   This knowledge is beauty.
It opens the soul of the land to

the creation of acceptance, of love,

        of Truth.

The water does not only see its own

path, its own journey

      but sees the destiny of all else.

The sky, the trees, the clouds,

the dirt, the creatures

      all see this unity.

I realized that I, too, knew of this river

      and that I was the one who had told the tale.

      But I had forgotten.

         I had left the memory.

      But this vision of water colliding

         and renewing its own pool—its own essence

reminded me of what I had forgotten—

      of what I had ceased to believe.

      This source of life is courage embodied.

It is love, peace, surrender, tranquility, unity.

It is the antiquity of the world.

      Ancient in its youth, it survives

         and gives life to all it touches.

      I have slept in the water's sunshine.

      I have felt the rays of warmth

         trickling down my very soul

      splashing into my heart

         and bringing light forth.

I step into the pool and feel the soft, cool
    water touching my soul.
    My toes slide down the water's edge
    and I splash my face of its clear essence.
I close my eyes and envision its beauty.
And it is beautiful.
    So pure in its actions—so true
        in its heart.
I slip further into the shadows
    and release my body to its warmth.
I feel its strength, its heart.
Before I know it I am fully immersed
    in its presence and I open
    my eyes and stare into its being.

I am reminded of an ancient tree.
    The alligator Juniper in its
        great mass rising from the
    dry soil—the hard-crusted earth.
Pure in sincerity, it offers me shade.
    The bark crawls up the trunk
        Like small, square creatures
        scaled like the fish of the water.
Its ancient source of life touches
the heart of birth.
The dust blows and clings to the rusty bark.

The branches bow to the sacredness
   of its principle art form:
               Life.
Hollowness it lives in but its grand
   posture fills the void of unknowing,
   of uncertainty.
Its austerity is joyful.
   the loneliness is long and perilous
      but the ties to the Holy Earth
   draw upon it compassion.
This compassion is its water.
   in the arid lands of loneliness.
The solemn cry of the Juniper
   no longer is in anguish
   but in peaceful existence.

Shana Lanzetta *currently lives in the Boston area. She is a music teacher and holds a master of music in choral conducting and a B.A. in secondary music education. She plans to soon attend the Interfaith Theological Seminary in Tucson, Arizona.*

Influences of mine . . .

One book: *The Diary of Anne Frank*

One album: Mozart's *Requiem*

One spiritual leader: My mother

One artist: Picasso

One thinker: Thich Nhat Hanh

13

Living at the Crossroads

EBOO PATEL

*J*ewish-American poet Kevin Coval says, a bit ruefully, "My hip-hop is better than my Hebrew." It's about the best metonym I've heard for my maligned and misrepresented generation. Kevin's mother sent him to Hebrew school in the swanky Chicago suburb where they lived, and he hated it. He told his rabbi that Jews were not the only Chosen People; they had to stop being consumed by their own suffering, and their obsession with status and wealth was impoverishing their souls. Kevin found a home in black-consciousness rap—Boogie Down Productions, Public Enemy, Arrested Development. In high school Kevin would quote from KRS One, "Some people call me a rap missionary, some people call me a walking dictionary, some people call me truly legendary, but what I really am is just a black revolutionary." (The absence of dusk in his skin tone didn't prevent him from feeling like a fellow soldier in the struggle.) Currently, Kevin teaches urban minority high school dropouts in Chicago, organizes art events for the Guild Complex, and writes and performs a jazz-influenced, hip-hop-based poetry.

Recently, Kevin has undertaken a serious study of Judaism. The focus on roots in rap sent him searching for his own. He meets regularly with a rabbi. Abraham is an important archetype in his poetry. He hosts Shabbat dinners and whispers Hebrew prayers when he breaks the bread. And when he *davens* (prays), he does it with *kavana* (right intention).

Kevin was born into the tradition of Judaism, and he ventured into the world of hip-hop. In his life, the two weave in and out of each other like a fugue. His involvement with hip-hop does not cause him to reject Judaism, only to rethink it.

My generation lives at the crossroads of inheritance and discovery. We are Muslims who admire the Dalai Lama and Christians who talk about karma. Our challenge is to be true to ancient traditions while living fully on the frontiers of modernity.

The Interfaith Youth Core is built at that intersection. We hold the space for the wisdom of ancient traditions, the reality of the modern world, and the hopes of young people to engage one another. The tie that binds these three entities is the desire for justice. The Prophets of the ancient traditions brought visions of justice, the sweatshops and environmental destruction of modernity demand justice, and young people are committed to working for justice. Our faith teaches us that the intention of the Creator is justice; our love works to bring Creation in line with it. The deal is there to be signed. The Interfaith Youth Core is committed to working out the details.

In the coming months, four of us who are called to this vision will create a community. We don't know where the money will come from. We don't have a Plan B. This skin-on-the-line commitment is the heart of the matter. The Interfaith Youth Core is not just an organization, it is a *sangha* (spiritual community) on pilgrimage. To live at the crossroads means to face inheritance and discovery fully, simultaneously.

We learn from those who have gone before: Dorothy Day, who asked the question "How should we try to live this life?" and provided an answer by the way she lived her own; Gandhi, who said, "Be the change you want to see in the world." Both emphasized that the core of their faith was working for justice. Both created communities where people lived out this vision. Both stood up to injustice within their own traditions. (Dorothy Day took on officials of the Catholic Church when she opposed Franco, and Gandhi watched the financial support of wealthy Hindus dry up when he held that the caste system had no place within Hinduism.) Both admired and learned from people of different traditions—Gandhi from Tolstoy, and Dorothy Day from Gandhi. We are not unique in saying we admire these leaders. But perhaps we seem a bit quaint when we seek to do something that resembles following their example.

Let me be frank: I am scared. The Trappist monk
Thomas Merton reminds us that true prayer requires great
courage because it demands change. As I open myself to
the light of Allah, what flaws will it reveal, what corrections
will it require? Injustice and despair are bottomless.
Heroes and prophets have come and gone; the poor are
still with us, and they are more ragged than ever. Can I face
the immensity of this injustice, call it my responsibility, and
taste the rust of my own powerlessness in the face of it?

What else is there to do but try? The idea is grand
and we are small. But once it has been considered, one cannot turn away. When Allah shines the light on a path, it is not
okay to pretend not to see it. The best we can do is to make
a start, and pray that God's grace helps us take the next
right step.

(Check out the Interfaith Youth Core at www.ifyc.org)

See page 4 for Eboo Patel's biographical information.

The Anti-Conclusion

JON M. SWEENEY,
EDITOR-IN-CHIEF, SkyLight Paths

*A*s you have by now seen and heard, this is not a collection of voices looking for tidy answers. Truth with a capital "T" has not only gone out of style—it just isn't very useful.

This is a generation, for lack of a better word, who will take us back to where spirituality most matters. They are less impressed with celebrities and slogans than their parents are, and more interested in what is most real.

They know that the future will hold whatever they put into it. And there is no shortage of challenges. Consider where we all have come from in the past century. A simple word-list of places and names speaks volumes:

- Hiroshima
- Auschwitz
- Mao
- Rwanda

- Pol Pot
- Vietnam
- Stalin
- Milosevic

And that is only a sampling of the highest profile, and most horrific, cases. But there is hope precisely because there are equally impressive human capacities for hope, goodness, redemption, and resistance. Another word-list—this time of names only:*

- Gandhi
- Black Elk
- Maha ghosananda
- Janusz Korczak
- Tutu
- Schweitzer
- Dorothy Day
- Dr. King
- Mother Teresa

Who will be the agents of spirituality in action in the future?

Today's new adults show us a world where our spiritual and religious traditions meet together at a very practical point—each with the potential of creating a better world from its central ideal. We can hope that in the future, deepening our spiritual lives will also mean rediscovering our traditions of karma yoga, *tikkun olam*, the Sermon on the Mount, and the bodhisattva vow, as we create our future together.

---

*For a complete and authoritative list of such people, see the forthcoming *Spiritual Innovators: 75 Spiritual People Who Changed the World in the Past Century*, ed. by Ira Rifkin and the editors at SkyLight Paths (SkyLight Paths, 2002).

About SKYLIGHT PATHS Publishing

SkyLight Paths Publishing is creating a place where people of different spiritual traditions come together for challenge and inspiration, a place where we can help each other understand the mystery that lies at the heart of our existence.

Through spirituality, our religious beliefs are increasingly becoming a part of our lives—rather than *apart* from our lives. While many of us may be more interested than ever in spiritual growth, we may be less firmly planted in traditional religion. Yet, we do want to deepen our relationship to the sacred, to learn from our own as well as from other faith traditions, and to practice in new ways.

SkyLight Paths sees both believers and seekers as a community that increasingly transcends traditional boundaries of religion and denomination—people wanting to learn from each other, *walking together, finding the way.*

We at SkyLight Paths take great care to produce beautiful books that present meaningful spiritual content in a form that reflects the art of making high quality books. Therefore, we want to acknowledge those who contributed to the production of this book.

PRODUCTION
Tim Holtz & Bridgett Taylor

EDITORIAL
Amanda Dupuis, Martha McKinney,
Polly Short Mahoney & Emily Wichland

COVER DESIGN
Tom Nihan, Gloucester, Massachusetts

INTERIOR DESIGN
Susan Ramundo, SR Desktop Services, Ridge, New York

PRINTING AND BINDING
Versa Press, East Peoria, Illinois

Other Interesting Books—Spirituality

Show Me Your Way
The Complete Guide to Exploring Interfaith Spiritual Direction
by *Howard A. Addison*

An ancient spiritual practice—reimagined for the modern seeker. Introduces people of all faiths—even those with no particular religious involvement—to the concept and practice of spiritual direction and, for the first time, to the dynamics of *interfaith* spiritual direction.
5½ x 8½, 208 pp, HC, ISBN 1-893361-12-8 **$21.95**

Waking Up: *A Week Inside a Zen Monastery*
by *Jack Maguire*; Foreword by *John Daido Loori, Roshi*

An essential guide to what it's like to spend a week inside a Zen Buddhist monastery.
6 x 9, 224 pp, b/w photographs, HC, ISBN 1-893361-13-6 **$21.95**

Making a Heart for God: *A Week Inside a Catholic Monastery*
by *Dianne Aprile*; Foreword by *Brother Patrick Hart, O.C.S.O.*

This essential guide to experiencing life in a Catholic monastery takes us to the Abbey of Gethsemani—the Trappist monastery in Kentucky that was home to author Thomas Merton—to explore the details. "This reviewer considers Aprile's work to be more balanced and informative than the popular *The Cloister Walk* by Kathleen Norris." —*Choice: Current Reviews for Academic Libraries*   6 x 9, 224 pp, b/w photographs, HC, ISBN 1-893361-14-4 $21.95

Come and Sit: *A Week Inside Meditation Centers*
by *Marcia Z. Nelson*

The insider's guide to meditation in a variety of different spiritual traditions. Traveling through Buddhist, Hindu, Christian, Jewish, and Sufi traditions, this essential guide takes the reader to different meditation centers to meet the teachers and students and learn about the practices, demystifying the meditation experience for people of all levels.

6 x 9, 224 pp, b/w photographs, Quality PB Original, ISBN 1-893361-35-7 **$16.95**

Or phone, fax, mail or e-mail to: SKYLIGHT PATHS Publishing
Sunset Farm Offices, Route 4 • P.O. Box 237 • Woodstock, Vermont 05091
Tel: (802) 457-4000   Fax: (802) 457-4004   www.skylightpaths.com
Credit card orders: (800) 962-4544 (9AM–5PM ET Monday–Friday)
Generous discounts on quantity orders. Satisfaction guaranteed. Prices subject to change.

Spirituality

Who Is My God?
An Innovative Guide to Finding Your Spiritual Identity
Created by *the Editors at SkyLight Paths*

Spiritual Type™ + Tradition Indicator = Spiritual Identity

Your Spiritual Identity is an undeniable part of who you are—whether you've thought much about it or not. This dynamic resource provides a helpful framework to begin or deepen your spiritual growth. Start by taking the unique Spiritual Identity Self-Test™; tabulate your results; then explore one, two or more of twenty-eight faiths/spiritual paths followed in America today. "An innovative and entertaining way to think—and rethink—about your own spiritual path, or perhaps even to find one." —Dan Wakefield, author of *How Do We Know When It's God?*
6 x 9, 160 pp, Quality PB Original, ISBN 1-893361-08-X **$15.95**

Spiritual Manifestos: *Visions for Renewed Religious Life in America from Young Spiritual Leaders of Many Faiths*
Edited by *Niles Elliot Goldstein*; Preface by *Martin E. Marty*

Discover the reasons why so many people have kept organized religion at arm's length.

Here, ten young spiritual leaders, most in their mid-thirties, representing the spectrum of religious traditions—Protestant, Catholic, Jewish, Buddhist, Unitarian Universalist—present the innovative ways they are transforming our spiritual communities and our lives. "These ten articulate young spiritual leaders engender hope for the vitality of 21st-century religion." —Forrest Church, Minister of All Souls Church in New York City
6 x 9, 256 pp, HC, ISBN 1-893361-09-8 **$21.95**

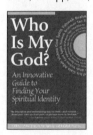 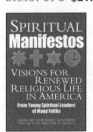  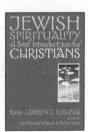

Jewish Spirituality: *A Brief Introduction for Christians*
by *Lawrence Kushner*

Lawrence Kushner, whose award-winning books have brought Jewish spirituality to life for countless readers of all faiths and backgrounds, tailors his unique style to address Christian's questions, revealing the essence of Judaism in a way that people whose own tradition traces its roots to Judaism can understand and enjoy. Offers Christian readers tools to strengthen their own faith. 5½ x 8½, 112 pp, Quality PB Original, ISBN 1-58023-150-0 **$12.95**

The Geography of Faith
Underground Conversations on Religious, Political, and Social Change
by *Robert Coles* and *Daniel Berrigan*; Updated foreword and afterword by the authors

A classic of faith-based activism—updated for a new generation.

Listen in on the conversations between these two great teachers—one a renegade priest wanted by the FBI for his protests against the Vietnam war, the other a future Pulitzer Prize winning journalist—as they struggle with what it means to put your faith to the test. Discover how their story of challenging the status quo during a time of great political, religious, and social change is just as applicable to our lives today. 6 x 9, 208 pp, Quality PB, ISBN 1-893361-40-3 **$16.95**

Other Interesting Books—Spirituality

How to Be a Perfect Stranger, In 2 Volumes
A Guide to Etiquette in Other People's Religious Ceremonies
Ed. by *Stuart M. Matlins* & *Arthur J. Magida* AWARD WINNERS!

Explains the rituals and celebrations of North America's major religions/denominations, helping an interested guest to feel comfortable, participate to the fullest extent possible, and avoid violating anyone's religious principles. Answers practical questions from the perspective of *any* other faith.

Vol. 1: North America's Largest Faiths
VOL. 1 COVERS: Assemblies of God • Baptist • Buddhist • Christian Church (Disciples of Christ) • Christian Science • Churches of Christ • Episcopalian/Anglican • Greek Orthodox • Hindu • Islam • Jehovah's Witnesses • Jewish • Lutheran • Methodist • Mormon • Presbyterian • Quaker • Roman Catholic • Seventh-day Adventist • United Church of Canada • United Church of Christ 6 x 9, 432 pp, Quality PB, ISBN 1-893361-01-2 **$19.95**

Vol. 2: More Faiths in North America
VOL. 2 COVERS: African American Methodist Churches • Baha'i • Christian and Missionary Alliance • Christian Congregation • Church of the Brethren • Church of the Nazarene • Evangelical Free Church • International Church of the Foursquare Gospel • International Pentecostal Holiness Church • Mennonite/Amish • Native American/First Nations • Orthodox Churches • Pentecostal Church of God • Reformed Church • Sikh • Unitarian Universalist • Wesleyan 6 x 9, 416 pp, Quality PB, ISBN 1-893361-02-0 **$19.95**

Prayer for People Who Think Too Much
A Guide to Everyday, Anywhere Prayer from the World's Faith Traditions
by *Mitch Finley*

Helps us make prayer a natural part of daily living.

Takes a thoughtful look at how each major faith tradition incorporates prayer into *daily* life. Explores Christian sacraments, Jewish holy days, Muslim daily prayer, "mindfulness" in Buddhism, and more, to help you better understand and enhance your own prayer practices. "I love this book." —Caroline Myss, author of *Anatomy of the Spirit*
5½ x 8½, 224 pp, Quality PB, ISBN 1-893361-21-7 **$16.95**; HC, ISBN 1-893361-00-4 **$21.95**

Or phone, fax, mail or e-mail to: SKYLIGHT PATHS Publishing
Sunset Farm Offices, Route 4 • P.O. Box 237 • Woodstock, Vermont 05091
Tel: (802) 457-4000 • Fax: (802) 457-4004 • www.skylightpaths.com
Credit card orders: (800) 962-4544 (9AM–5PM ET Monday–Friday)
Generous discounts on quantity orders. Satisfaction guaranteed. Prices subject to change.